SIU 101

Special Investigation Units:

Guidelines, Formats, Procedures,
Forms and Philosophy
For Investigators and Adjustors

by
Bill Kizorek and Scott Finger

PUBLICATIONS

1163 E. Ogden Avenue • Suite 705-360
Naperville, Illinois 60563
(708) 955-0940

The information and guidelines contained in this book have been gathered by interviews and correspondence with many of the most well-known Special Investigation Unit (SIU) directors and their top investigators. Because courts and legislatures around the country are constantly updating the rules, it is critical that SIU staffers are conversant with local regulations. This book is not an attempt in any way to provide legal advice, but merely offers claims investigators guidelines and references to use as a starting point in identifying and investigating potentially fraudulent claims.

Produced and Designed by Debra Martino

Illustrated by Al Ochsner

Printed in China

ISBN 1-884230-03-2

Table of Contents

Introduction

This book is for special investigators or adjusters who want to become more conversant with what goes into making a fraud investigation. By the way, the word *fraud* should not be taken lightly. Fraud is a serious accusation of criminal or civil wrongdoing.

The majority of questionable insurance claims are not actually fraudulent but may contain inconsistencies and exaggerations. Although an investigation for fraud may not result in prosecution, that same investigation may uncover information that will result in a significant reduction in indemnity dollar payout.

All insurance investigators, especially SIU personnel, must be fair and impartial throughout the entire fact-gathering process. The guidelines and procedures contained in this book should help the investigator efficiently and methodically develop information in a way that is both ethical and protective of the rights of claimants.

Premium Fraud may be present if too many File Clerks are falling off of roofs.

SIU 101: Kizorek/Finger

Insurance Fraud Areas

There is potentially fraudulent activity throughout the entire spectrum of the insurance business. Some SIU operatives specialize in one of the areas, while others are generalists investigating in many of the realms. Here is an overview of how fraud may rear its ugly head in this business.

WORKER'S COMPENSATION

Workers may collect total disability payments by alleging that they are unable to work and, at the same time, may be working elsewhere. More often than working, the disabled workers are found performing physical activities that would indicate they are much more healthy than alleged. The majority of worker's compensation SIU investigations should end up in a settled file instead of in prosecution. The savings in indemnity dollars not paid out is an important justification for the continued funding of SIU programs by insurers.

PREMIUM FRAUD

In worker's compensation, you also will be exposed to premium fraud and medical provider fraud. In the former, the insured may classify employees in a way that deceives the insurer and results in a reduction of premium. When the insurer begins to notice that 14 different file clerks fell off of roofs and two secretaries fell off ladders during the course of their employment, it might be a good time to visit the insured and see how accurate the job descriptions were. Some employers will use employee leasing companies to accomplish the same premium reduction.

MEDICAL PROVIDER FRAUD

Medical provider fraud involves unscrupulous doctors, chiropractors and other medical personnel who actually encourage the filing of claims and often create tens of thousands of dollars of medical bills (therapy, adjustments, massages, medication) on a case where little or no treatment was needed.

AUTOMOBILES

Vehicles reported stolen that were not really stolen are a problem area. Torch jobs, "paper cars," cars ending up in the bottom of quarries and cars delivered to chop shops always are areas of fraud investigation. Almost two million vehicles a year are stolen. The NICB in Palos Heights, Illinois is by far the most important agency spearheading an industry drive against automobile fraud. Call the bureau at 1-800-TEL-NICB.

One special interest to fraud investigators working the automobile detail is the export of stolen vehicles. Many of the cars stolen in the United States end up in the cargo holds of ships heading off for foreign ports. Once a Firebird makes it to Panama, it is unlikely that it will ever be rediscovered.

PROPERTY

Arson, burglary and false-contents filings on homeowners' claims are some of the many areas in which fraud investigations may uncover wrongdoing. Business owners may report fire, smoke, water damage or theft of out-of-date, unsaleable or excess inventory or supplies.

Going Overboard

Energy and aggressiveness are commendable in a potential fraud investigation. Overzealousness, on the other hand, may expose you and your employer to problems the SIU director would rather not have to confront.

Keep in mind that the vast majority of claims investigations are probes into the legitimacy of a contract your company has made with a person or organization. You are, for the most part, conducting a business transaction. Act business-like.

In the course of an investigation that is beginning to turn up questionable behavior, it is human nature to get excited and engage in practices that, when viewed later by a jury of six or twelve *reasonable* citizens, may appear unacceptably aggressive or intrusive. As these investigations progress, the following tips will go a long way in helping you avoid problems.

- Do not be malicious or abusive.

- Do not be overzealous.

- Do not overlook exculpatory evidence as you gather incriminating evidence.

- Disseminate information only to those:
  a. who have a need to know.
  b. who have a legitimate interest in the investigation.
  c. who can help you with your investigation.

- Do not use an SIU investigation as a threat to pressure for a settlement of the claim.

- Conduct the investigation in a reasonable fashion.

- Always remember, a person who files a claim sacrifices a certain amount of their right to privacy. Those claimants however, do have a "reasonable expectation of privacy" that should always be kept in mind.

Special investigators should always remember
to keep their work business-like and on
a professional level.

Bad Faith Fever

Want to see the temperature rise in the office of the Vice-President of Claims? Present him with a bundle of *bad faith* lawsuits that are indefensible. The courts have occasionally looked unkindly upon insurers who have, in *the courts* mind, treated claimants in a callous, insensitive, unreasonable manner. When a few insurers did not act in *good faith*, they were nailed with gaspingly high punitive damages. Not only did many insurers gasp, but so did hundreds of plaintiff attorneys as they ran to court staking their claims. Having incubated in a certain large west coast state that began with the letter "C," the bad faith assault on insurers was labeled the "New California Gold Rush."

Early on, some insurers were the target of many bad faith threats. It seemed an appropriate additional threat to gain leverage in the claim. Why risk a ten million dollar bad faith verdict by denying a lousy $20,000 fire claim? But as more cases for bad faith went to court, a certain amount of reason began to return to the process. Courts began to say, "Wait a second, if an insurer is deprived of its right to dispute a claim, the costs to society would be overwhelming." As a result, many bad faith suits ended up being dismissed through pretrial motions.

Although claims staff should be aware that a true bad faith claims procedure might land them a slot on CNN Headline News, attention to some simple standards will eliminate any potentially successful bad faith tort. Here is the solution: *be reasonable.* Here is what not to be: unreasonable, capricious, reckless; don't ignore, delay, or deny a claim that may be valid without good reason.

Douglas G. Houser, an attorney from Portland, Oregon, did extensive legal research into this subject. According to Mr. Houser, "Often a subjective element is required to determine whether the insurer, in bad faith, denied or delayed payment of a claim. Claimants must prove the insurer's blameworthy state of mind in denying or delaying payment. The courts have recognized that insurers have a duty to question appropriate claims and that there is no duty to pay claims for which there is no coverage."

So what does this all boil down to? Go ahead and question those claims that look suspicious. Make sure you document *why* there was reasonable suspicion to delay or deny. If you have a prima facie case laden with reasonableness there will be less chance that a bad faith action will get off the ground. Use red flags, evidence and have at least a reasonable argument for questioning the claim.

Reasonable. Unreasonable. Sorry to lean on those words so heavily, but that is what bad faith is all about. The courts have clearly acknowledged your right to investigate. Do not be intimidated from conducting a thorough investigation simply because you are being accused of bad faith. Treat claimants fairly and with dignity. Do not wear your "Fraud Busters" T-shirt to the interview.

Testifying

Testifying is a way of life for many SIU operatives. The information gathered will be presented to the courts through depositions or testimony before the courts. At times, this testimony will be given in the face of hostility, especially in the face of a claimant's attorney who may lose tens of thousands of dollars (or more) in contingency fees because of the investigator's work.

Before appearing to testify, there is one important issue you will want to clear up with the counsel for your company. Who do you say you work for? Although the answer would seem to be rudimentary, there is some amount of risk in automatically responding with the name of your employer in the middle of jury trial testimony. The very mention of the presence of an insurance company investigator may result in a mistrial. Although juries may assume that insurance is involved, there might be a tendency for a higher verdict if they knew for certain that the multibillion dollar treasury of a major insurance company was available to raid.

The testimony itself can be a real drama. You may be up against an eloquent and highly paid plaintiff's attorney, or even a criminal defense attorney. Either one will be looking after their client's best interests and if it means ripping off your flesh, pecking out your eyeballs and ripping your bones apart (figuratively speaking, of course), so be it. There will be a special attempt to determine if you are hiding information that you uncovered in your investigation which may help the defendant.

A book devoted to testifying in insurance claims cases, *Greenhorn Witness*, by Bill Kizorek, takes a nuts-and-bolts approach to the art of testifying. With permission from the author, here are some excerpts from the book:

> You, the witness, are the centerpiece. All are gathered to hear your
> story so that facts of the case are known before the actual trial. You are

Although it is rare, the SIU Investigator will be called to testify. Preparation for the event is critical.

SIU 101: Kizorek/Finger

expected to tell what you know of the facts, to the best of your knowledge as you remember it on the particular day of the deposition.

Documents, notes: You may have received a subpoena to bring certain documents. Bring the subpoena along with the documents. Review those documents prior to the deposition to refresh your memory. Anything you refer to during the deposition may be taken out of your hands by the plaintiff's attorney and either examined or entered as an official court exhibit. Also, if you read from a notebook, the entire notebook may be taken from you and perused by the opposing attorney (even if only one page refers to the case at hand).

Memorizing: don't. If you need facts or statements, bring them in. If you try to memorize too many things, you may become confused or give the wrong information.

Beforehand: Before a deposition, it is permissible and often advisable to meet with your attorney and discuss the matter in advance. It also is acceptable practice to admit to these meetings when asked about them by the plaintiff's attorney.

TESTIMONY

Testifying at a deposition can be similar to giving testimony at trial. Let's get right into the procedures using the deposition as the setting. It begins with your being sworn in as a witness. When you are asked by the court reporter if you do "solemnly swear to tell the truth, the whole truth," etc., answer loud and clearly, "I do."

By the way, note the word "solemnly." Keep it in mind. Depositions are serious legal meetings. Financial fortunes, even people's livelihoods, are at stake. This is not the time to joke around. But do not be so constrained that you feel uncomfortable. Relax and act natural.

THE INTERROGATION

It may sound less intimidating to say "questioning," but it really is more than a tea party with pleasant questions and answers. Fur may fly, especially if the plaintiff's attorney feels that you are hedging, not telling the full truth, slanting your story to benefit the defense, forgetting too much, selectively remembering or not telling the truth.

Testifying at a trial is a lot like giving a deposition.
When giving your answers, face the jury or,
if only a judge is present, face that judge.

You might sail through the deposition so smoothly that you will wonder what all the fuss and bother was about. Then again, it might be like trying to sail though a storm, getting hit by verbal lightning bolts and trying to avoid running up onto a reef. The best course is to prepare yourself to be thoroughly examined and be mentally strong enough to pull through.

Knowing in advance how to field tough or confusing questions will be 90 percent of the battle. There is no telling what specific questions will be asked or how a simple question might be asked in a complex or confusing way. Remember that your questioner is not only looking for the truth, but also for any way to promote the case on behalf of the client.

Here, then, are some time-tested hints on how to testify, both in a deposition as well as in a courtroom. A thorough knowledge of this advice will enhance your value as a witness who is knowledgeable, honest and serving the cause of truth and justice.

1. **Listen Carefully.**

    A. Pause before answering. Think.

    B. Understand the question completely.

    C. Do not answer any question unless you understand it.

    D. If a question is vague or confusing, ask the examiner to restate or clarify it.

2. **Keep Your Answers Simple.**

    A. Answer yes or no whenever possible.

    B. Do not elaborate unless clarification is necessary.

    C. Do not volunteer information.

3. **Give Definitive Answers.**

    A. Do not exaggerate.

    B. Answers should be short, well thought out.

4. **Keep Cool.**

    A. Do not be a wise guy, sarcastic or combative.

    B. Do not be "rattled" by the questioning procedure.

    C. Do not be intimidated.

When testifying, don't let the opposing
attorney put words in your mouth.

SIU 101: Kizorek/Finger

5. **Be Truthful, Always.**

   A. It is OK to say, "I don't know."

   B. It is OK to say, "That's all I remember."

   C. It is OK to say, "To the best of my knowledge."

6. **Watch for Warning Signs That You Are Getting Worn Down.**

   A. Watch for fatigue, anger, short temper, impatience.

   B. Request a "short break" if necessary.

   C. Avoid rushing testimony just to "get out of there."

7. **Don't Let the Opposing Attorney "Put Words in Your Mouth."**

   A. Be alert for comparisons or analogies.

   B. Be alert for "trick questions."

   C. Be alert for different wording of the same question.

   D. If you feel the attorney is not letting you answer correctly, make a statement to that effect for the record.

8. **Always review any documents presented to you.**

   A. Thoroughly read the entire document.

   B. Look for any changes that may have been made since you last reviewed it.

   C. If you are not familiar with the document and you feel you must offer an opinion, fully understand its contents before offering any opinion.

IN THE COURTROOM

Testifying in court can in many instances be similar to testifying during a deposition. Many of the principles are the same, especially your demeanor and presence of mind while being questioned "on the stand." But there are more people: the judge, jury (sometimes), courtroom staff, even an audience. Consequently, there may be more pressure and drama. There are differences to be aware of. While in the courtroom, the way you appear will be more of a factor than it was during the deposition. The way you present yourself also will help (or hinder) your acceptance as a believable witness.

TRICK QUESTIONS SECTION

The plaintiff's attorney has been hired to protect the interests of the client. To that end, the attorney will use any number of techniques to elicit a response from you that will be favorable to the client's case. You may have exact knowledge of the facts, but two different attorneys may have you express those facts in ways that look opposite from one another. Be prepared to have questions thrown at you that will expose you to an answer that does not convey what you want.

It may be unfair to categorize these interrogative techniques as "trick questions," but it is obvious that the phrase has developed over time as a result of countless witnesses feeling that they had been "tricked" into saying something they did not mean. So let's call them trick questions and take a look at some of the angles.

The question: "Is this true? Just answer yes or no!"

Your response: "I cannot answer with a simple yes or no."

Secondary response: If the plaintiff's attorney persists, you may say, "To answer yes or no would be misleading."

The question: "Wouldn't you agree that …?"

Your response: Watch out! The plaintiff's attorney may be setting you up to agree to something that will prove his or her point but not relate to the testimony you have given. If the question seems faulty or is difficult to understand, have the attorney repeat it. If it is still not in a form you can answer, you can say, "I don't understand the question."

The question: "Have you spoken to the defense attorney about this matter before you testified? If so, what did he or she tell you to say?"

Your response: "Yes. The attorney asked me about the facts and told me to tell the truth in all matters." (There are a wide variety of answers you can give, but do not be afraid to admit to having discussed the case prior to your testimony.)

The question: "How much are you being paid to testify for the defense?"

Your response: Pause for a moment to give the defense an opportunity to object. If there is no objection, go ahead and answer. If you are simply on the

There are times when testifying
can be a memorable experience.

payroll of your company and are testifying, you may answer that the company is paying your regular salary. If you are being paid a fee as a professional expert witness, you may mention the amount you are charging, or state your usual "hourly rates."

The question: "Have you ever lied?"

Your response: "Yes, but never under oath."

The question: "Would you say that what you have told me is the same as …?"

Your response: Alert! Here is the "putting the words in your mouth" scenario to watch out for. Do not get sucked into agreeing to analogies or comparisons that may take your observations and twist them to mean something they do not. Do not be afraid to challenge the comparison; do it politely.

The question: "Are you telling me …?

Your response: Beware! Watch the rewording to make certain that the words are not being twisted to change the meaning to serve the interests of the plaintiff. Be prepared to say, "I'm not telling you that." You then may repeat your own statement the way it was meant to be expressed. Another motive is that the plaintiff's attorney may want you to change your answer to one that is more acceptable to the plaintiff's position.

In the end, the mandate is that the truth be presented. You, as the fraud investigator, should be prepared enough so that the truth of your testimony is not negatively manipulated by a skillful opposing attorney. This preparation, when combined with incontrovertible factual evidence, will guarantee that justice prevails.

Greenhorn Witness, paperback, is available from PSI Publications, 1163 East Ogden, Naperville, Illinois 60563, for $9.95 plus $2.00 for shipping and handling.

Surveillance

Video surveillance is an indispensable tool for claims fraud investigations. This chapter specifically addresses the SIU use of surveillance in bodily injury investigations.

OUTSIDE VENDOR VERSUS IN-HOUSE SURVEILLANTS

It is no secret that the authors of this book are executives of an independent surveillance company. One, however (Finger), spent several years at a private surveillance company, then a couple more as an SIU investigator at a national insurance company before returning to the private investigation field. The wisdom that follows attempts to strike a balance between the use of in-house surveillants and outside vendors.

The biggest plus for in-house surveillance facilities is the convenience of having the person on staff, in addition to the consistency of the work product, the economy (if there are enough cases in the immediate area) and the direct supervision of the work product.

But the majority of SIU surveillances are sent to independent agencies to be investigated. Many SIU directors want to use their budgets for staff and not equipment. At the authors' company, at the time of this book's publication, it was costing about $950,000 per month to run 70 surveillance vans, including 30 other vehicles and a support staff of 75.

Training and licensing (state by state) are other nettlesome issues, as well as supervision. Also, because of SIU investigator caseloads, the proper amount of time needed for an effective surveillance cannot always be given to each individual assignment. This analysis of the use of surveillance, for simplicity's sake, will assume the work is being done by an outside vendor. The principles and theories are easily applied to in-house surveillance investigators.

PROBLEMS, PROBLEMS, PROBLEMS

- Investigators get caught.

- Investigators lose the subject they are following.

- Investigators film the wrong person.

It would be a more pleasant world for vendors if clients had a better understanding that these three things happen. What else?

- Claimants sometimes look injured.

- Claimants sometimes never leave the house.

- Claimants sometimes are not even inside the house.

- Claimants sometimes leave out the backdoor and walk.

- Claimants sometimes start every day looking for you.

- Claimants sometimes drive like lunatics.

But that, of course, is not all.

- Some residences have four exits.

- Sometimes, there is no accurate subject description.

- There may be no vehicle description or tag numbers.

- Fifty people may live in the subject's building.

- A surveillants nightmare: all of the above on one case.

Welcome to the harsh realities of surveillance.

It is imperative that the difficulties of surveillance are understood by those who buy the services. It also is critical that those of us supervisors lucky enough to be wearing white shirts and ties as we swivel around in our leather Knoll office chairs (authors sometimes included) remember just how tough it is out there on the streets. These claimants have not invited us, do not in any way cooperate and sometimes fire .38 caliber bullets through the thin metal walls of the van.

Proceed, now, to the nuts-and-bolts section of this business.

STARTING TIMES

Early, early, early! If the subject is a disabled tradesman such as a carpenter, start very early. On the first day of surveillance, the average case should have

Surveillance Nightmare: Seventeen-story building, four exits, no vehicle and no decent physical description.

On surveillance, if you want to see the claimant leave, just go out and order a triple cheeseburger with a jumbo scalding coffee. Take the lid off the coffee and eat the first bite of your cheeseburger. Get catchup and mustard all over your hands. At this point, the claimant will pull out of the garage.

get to the corner, the retired police sergeant crossing guard is holding up a neon portable stop sign in your face as seven angelic neighborhood children, spread out five feet apart, dance across the intersection. When you finally get to the main artery, the claimant has made a right (or was it a left?) turn and inserted the Z-28 into a line of 60 other cars. *Adios*.

This is the world of surveillance. There is no option. The claimant leaves; you follow. If that claimant is a 62 year-old lady driving a four-door, 15 year-old New Yorker, the procedure is more soothing: Turn on some classical music, sit back and follow her from one store to another.

If the claimant is a 23 year-old gypsy roofer driving a red Firebird, fasten your safety belt, toss the hot coffee out, throw the cup in the back of your vehicle and prepare for a possible ride from hell.

About safety: It comes first. Safety comes before keeping clients happy. It is paramount even if the trial begins the next morning and this is your last day on the case. It comes first even if your boss says that he or she will fire you if you lose the gypsy roofer one more time. (Invite your boss to take the wheel.)

Losing the claimant: It happens. Some clients want you to quit on the spot and go home. A better technique is to search for the claimant for at least an hour in the most likely places. Half the time, claimants seem to return home within a couple of hours. Use investigative ingenuity; guess where that person is going. Perform a "grid search," driving up and down the streets in the area where the claimant was last observed. Follow up on information provided by the insured, claims staff and rehabilitation reports. If the claimant was said to play golf, check out the local driving ranges.

Getting caught: It happens. Just start the morning with more gas in your tank than the claimant has in his or hers. Do not discuss the case with the subject. In many states, it is against the law to share information about a surveillance with anyone other than the client and local law enforcement. Sharing information with the claimant, although seemingly a good idea when he or she is holding a chain-saw blade against your neck, is an especially bad idea. Avoid confrontation at all costs. If trapped, just tell the claimant that you would be happy to discuss matters with the local police chief in attendance, "because the chief knows I'm out here right now." Do what is needed to get out of the pickle of you versus the claimant, one on one (or worse, you versus six crowbar-wielding gypsy roofers).

During surveillance, choices are difficult. You do not want to get caught; you do not want to lose the claimant. The closer you get while following, the more likely you will get caught. The further you stay back, the more likely you will lose the claimant. Regardless of what you do, remember this: Your boss or client always will have a better perspective on how you *should have* worked the case! Also, lose two different claimants for the same client and the client may abandon you for another agency that in all likelihood also will lose claimants during the course of its investigations.

VIDEOTAPING

You are an unbiased witness, a collector of facts. When observing claimant activity, tape everything. If a claimant digs holes for two hours then smokes a cigarette for ten minutes, film it all. Do not edit out anything because you feel it might hurt the case. Film activity. Film inactivity. If you end up with eight hours of film, you always can prepare an edited tape for doctors, arbitrators or other hearings officers. But the unedited tape always should be made known and available if needed during negotiation, hearings or arbitration proceedings.

Using Tapes Once You Get Them

There is a split discussion here: Are the films going to be used for prosecution or to mitigate the indemnity payments on the file? By far, the great majority of all tapes will be used as an intrinsic part of the claim adjustment process. Although the number is increasing, less than 2 percent of tapes will go to prosecution (based on the authors' experience with tens of thousands of surveillances). Most will be used by the adjusters to come to a fair settlement of the personal-injury action.

In this setting, the SIU investigator should realize that the great value of the evidence is to compare the allegations of disability to the reality of the videotaped activity. In the vast majority of personal-injury claims where significant physical activity has been recorded, the videotapes are going to show that the claimant exaggerated his disability.

More often than not, the use of videotapes will decrease the payout of indemnity dollars to the claimant, who probably will not be the subject of a fraud prosecution.

The following information should allow the SIU investigator to guide and inform the claims adjustor in the effective use of videotapes as evidence. When used properly, videotape evidence can be an extremely useful tool in evaluating the extent of injury of a liability or worker's compensation claimant.

The first step in determining the value of videotape as a settlement tool is to compare the claimant's physical activity that was documented via surveillance with his or her allegations of disability as well as doctor-imposed restrictions. If there are no indications that the claimant was aware of the

An effective strategy with videotapes is to withhold divulging the contents until you have deposed (or redeposed) the claimant.

surveillance and appeared to be injured or acting in a manner that would be consistent with the alleged injury, then the injury may, in fact, be legitimate. Knowledge of this could lead the adjustor to settle the claim in a more timely fashion with a clear conscience that fraud was possibly not involved.

On the other hand, if the physical activity recorded on the videotape shows that the extent of injury may be exaggerated, the video (when used properly) will be of great benefit in decreasing potential payout exposure and coming to a fair settlement for both the insurance company and the claimant.

For SIU personnel as well as claims adjustors to properly use videotapes as evidence, the following suggestions should be kept in mind:

Rule 1: Videotape all activity and never edit or tamper with the contents of the original tape, which must remain intact. A short-version videotape, however, showing highlights of documented physical activity should be brought to the trial or hearing because of time constraints of arbitrators, judges and other involved personnel. The court should be provided with both the original and edited tapes as evidence.

Rule 2: When showing videotape evidence to doctors and physicians, show the edited version (unless otherwise requested) and advise them that the tape has been edited. Videotapes may change the opinion of the claimant's doctor or reinforce the opinion of the independent medical examiner. Be sure you know and understand the rules in the state which you are operating in regarding "ex parte" communication (conversation with claimant's physician that is not in the presence of claimant's attorney) before approaching the claimant's physician. Such discussions may be precluded in certain states.

Rule 3: Inconsistency is the key issue when using videotape as a settlement tool. If the tapes show that the claimant's allegations of disability are not consistent with the documented physical activity, the credibility of the claimant is then in question.

Rule 4: Do not disclose the full contents of the videotapes to the claimant or his or her attorney immediately. In many instances, the claimants and their counsel have redesigned the injury to fit the contents of the videotape.

Rule 5: If the videotapes are requested by the claimant's attorney through discovery motions, it may be advantageous to request a discovery deposition prior to disclosing the contents of the video. This has become an accepted strategy in attempting to preserve the integrity and impeachment value of the evidence. It should be noted that state rules vary regarding the ability to take a second deposition of a claimant, so before requesting a discovery deposition (if the claimant has previously been deposed), make certain that option is available in your area of operation.

Rule 6: In those jurisdictions where thorough pretrial discovery is an accepted procedure, not only should the investigator be listed as a witness, but the existence of the videotapes should be revealed.

Rule 7: The investigator testifying on a surveillance case should be an objective and impartial observer and should not appear to have an "ax to grind." The investigator also should review any notes, reports and the videotape prior to the hearing to be fully prepared for testimony.

Rule 8: The vast majority of claims involving strenuous physical activity on tape will settle prior to trial. The most significant value is that video-taped activity tends to bring the claimant and his or her attorney into a more settlement-thinking frame of mind.

Rule 9: Before any decisions are made regarding discontinuing benefits, an effort should be made to get an independent confirmation of the identity of the subject. Video snips can be pulled from the surveillance tape and shown to individuals who will be able to establish that the person on the videotape is, in fact, the claimant. Sources could include rehabilitation staff, adjustors, claimant's supervisors at the workplace, defense attorneys, doctors or even an independent medical exam (IME). Before contacting a claimant's physician, please make certain that the rules of your state allow you to do so. Certain state statutes regarding "ex parte" conversations may preclude you from approaching a claimant's physician for purposes of identification.

Special Investigation Unit/ Vendor Relationships

The SIU investigator must be in contact with many individuals. This may include claimants, law-enforcement, fire investigators, attorneys, fraud bureaus, claims adjustors, management, and outside vendors. In the past a lot of this contact was with claim department staffers deeply immersed in the issues of professional claim handling.

Because so many of the SIU ranks are being filled by ex-law enforcement officers, there has been a change in some of the business relationships with other professionals. Within the ranks of surveillance companies, for instance, there has been some concern that, as SIU supervisors take over the management of surveillance, some of them put an emphasis on dollar-per-hour fees and less concern on the quality of work product, supervision, and internal controls by the vendors.

There should be as much of a balance as is possible in this subjective business. The airlines competed against each other in costs until the industry was decimated by bankruptcy and lower standards of service. SIU management should be cautious about dismantling the existing system of vendors for the purposes of getting it done the cheapest way possible. Ultimately a well managed, properly equipped, professionally staffed vendor will be in a better position to enhance the performance of the SIU itself. A vendor who is a respected partner in the fraud fighting program will be the kind of ally that the in-house investigator can depend on to help in the overall battle. Although there are times that SIU staff have been tough to deal with, it is also incumbent on the vendor to prove to the SIU that the rates charged are justified by the "value-added" features of the service provided.

A good working relationship between SIU staffers and vendors can lead to better results.

Managing the Vendor

Vendors want to perform to the client's satisfaction. Sometimes, they fall short. Reasons may include a poorly trained staff, insufficient surveillance equipment, too busy, disorganized, undercapitalized or just plain inefficient. Just as the best managers are the ones that tell their people what they want and guide them through it, so, too, the best clients are those who clearly outline their needs to the vendor and give the vendor a chance to change or improve. An effective, well-run outside surveillance vendor can be a long-term partner making the SIU look good. Ways to cement this relationship include:

- Tell the vendor when something does not appear to be correct.

- Give the vendor a chance to improve.

- Understand the difficulties of surveillance.

- Do not drive the vendor's rates down to the point that he or she cannot afford professional staff, proper supervision and adequate insurance coverage. If unusually low bids come in, be suspect.

Basic prerequisites for a surveillance company are:

- Ongoing training programs for investigative staff;

- State license in each state working;

- Insurance: professional liability, worker's compensation, automobile;

- Equipment. To this day, there are surveillance companies working out of cars with cameras perched on investigators' shoulders. This is not the way to do it. Proper equipment includes unassuming, well-maintained vehicles, state-of-the-art videocameras, and a heavy-duty tripod that will help avoid any shake or movement when filming.

The use of outside vendors is sometimes akin to walking through a mine field: Improper insurance, licensing or supervision could blow up into a major problem.

With the influx of SIU staff members from outside of the insurance and management ranks, there also has come somewhat of an impatient, "I can do it better than you" approach to managing vendors. It would be better for both the SIU and vendors if the relationship were more a partnership and less a competition.

What Might Go Wrong

Fraud investigations are fraught with difficulties. Bad faith, harassment, surveillance of the wrong person, lack of claimant cooperation, cantankerous attorneys – these are just some of the land mines to beware of. On the other hand, SIU investigators and claim-department adjusters have a fiduciary responsibility to protect the assets of the insurer. The claimants also have rights. SIU investigators must find the proper balance between getting to the truth but doing so in a way that is fair to both sides.

Overzealous investigations can lead to charges of harassment and persecution. More than a couple of these accusations for a local SIU office might prompt closer scrutiny of the investigative methods being used and may even lead to a liability situation for the claims department.

SIU staffers must be conversant with statutory procedures, such as the length of time allowed for a reasonable investigation. Several states, such as California, mandate certain time schedules. If a claim has to be evaluated in a certain period of time, fraud investigators must be sensitive to those deadlines.

Surveillance is an area where things go wrong with regularity. Investigators lose claimants, they get caught and they film the wrong person. This happens to the best of investigators. Clients must be made aware that these things may occur even when the most veteran investigators are involved.

Most important is that special care must be taken before benefits are denied or criminal charges filed. Remember, the surveillance investigator cannot simply go up to the claimant at the end of the day and ask for an identification (ID) card. As always, confirming the identification of claimants is of the utmost importance prior to any action taken on a file because of the existence of surveillance videotapes.

Invasion of privacy is always an issue to contend with. If an investigator goes up to a neighbor's house and says that he or she "thinks that Mr. Williams burned his house down," the investigator may be opening a can of worms. An investigator, as well, should not be sorting through a claimant's mailbox.

Fairness to claimants should be the compelling rule of thumb. If you respect their rights to privacy and treat them fairly, it is unlikely that post-investigative trouble will ensue.

SIU Investigator/Claims Adjustor Relationships

In many insurance companies, the individual most important to the success of a Special Investigation Unit is the claims adjustor. The adjustor can be considered the second line of defense in fighting potentially fraudulent claims if one considers that if properly trained, the insured can also recognize signs that something may be amiss in a particular file.

In the majority of instances, however, it is the adjustors who must take it upon themselves to identify suspicious claims, then follow up with a referral to the SIU for further investigation. Once the file has been given over to the SIU, the adjustor still must pass along any new information or occurrences pertinent to the file, such as telephone calls from the claimant, new addresses, scheduled appointments or independent medical exams (IMEs) and even notifying the investigator if the claim has been settled or dropped during the course of the investigation.

After completing the investigation, the adjustor must review the gathered information and decide on how to proceed on the file. Decisions include determining whether the investigation shows improper or fraudulent behavior, what steps must be taken to properly handle the file (possibly including further investigation), how to use the evidence to settle the claim, if there needs to be attorney involvement and if claim dollars already have been paid out can any recovery action be taken.

The SIU investigator can use his or her expertise throughout this process, counseling the adjustor in what is believed to be the best way to handle the file. This continuous interface will result not only in a claims adjustor more aware of insurance fraud and the steps needed to ensure a proper investigation, but also a claims adjustor who is more likely to increase the volume of referrals to the SIU unit.

Training claims staff members through fraud seminars, distributing lists of red flags that indicate potentially fraudulent behavior, handing out articles concerning fraud and also giving word of prosecutions or savings made through investigation always will be an important part of the SIU staffer's job. More important, however, is the daily interaction during the course of an investigation between the adjustor and the investigator.

Ride-along programs can also be very helpful in educating claims staff in the daily activities of an SIU investigator. An adjustor who has participated in a ride-along will better understand not only the amount of time it takes to properly investigate a claim, but also some of the many difficulties encountered daily during the course of evaluating the merits of that claim. Before setting up a ride-along program, be certain that insurance company policy and SIU guidelines allow for that type of activity.

Working closely together not only will allow for better communication regarding the file, but will build confidence in the adjustor that the SIU department is an integral part of the claims-handling process.

Fraud Training/Speech Giving by the Investigator

Identifying fraudulent activity is just one part of the overall duty of the special investigator. To effectively combat the overall problem of insurance fraud, the investigator also must be a communicator – informing not only other insurance company departments, but also the general public. The more society understands that insurance fraud affects *everyone*, the greater will be the support for claims investigative operations.

Although the majority of investigators are expert at probing, it is not so probable that the investigator is an expert in the art of public speaking.

The strategies and techniques of this chapter will help the fraud investigator prepare a polished, professional, convincing and, at times, *entertaining* presentation. Just because the message is a serious one does not mean that conveying that message has to be a somber affair.

PREPARATION

The single most important success factor is thorough preparation. Not only should the investigator have a complete grasp of his or her subject matter (assumed), but gathering other information should be part of the process: Who is the audience, what are its interests, what is its focus, are audiovisual materials needed and will the proper equipment be available? It is easier to request that an overhead projector be made available for your speech than to haul one around yourself.

PRACTICE – PRACTICE – PRACTICE

The more thoroughly you have rehearsed your presentation, the less you have to worry about nervousness. This will give you the time that is demanded for concentrating on presentation techniques. Unless protocol dictates otherwise, get your speech down to a five-inch by seven-inch note card with key words. Twenty to thirty key words written on a card, each word symbolizing a section of your speech, will free up your eyes to roam across the audience. Take the note card and practice the speech. Practice it out loud. Give the speech again. Give it in front of whoever will listen to you before your major performance. Accept any criticism as constructive and solicit advice from your small audience. During your dry runs, stop anytime and go back over the sentence until you get it the correct way, inflection and all.

SPEECH DAY

Start the day with a good night's sleep under your belt. In addition, too much alcohol the night before will slow down the motors of your brain, even for a lunchtime speech on the following day.

Your brain loves protein so go ahead and eat something in the morning. Presuming that it is a luncheon speech, eat sparingly just before the speech. The more food you cram into your stomach, the more blood will be diverted to help digest the food. You need as much circulation as possible going to your brain.

Get to the location of your speech at least 30 minutes in advance. Check out the audiovisual equipment, not only to see that it is *physically* there, but also that it is operational. Go up to the microphone and make sure it works. Adjust it. Say a couple sentences of your speech into it (if no one is around yet). If your presentation calls for the dimming of lights, by all means ensure that those lights *can* be dimmed. It is not only advisable to have a light dimmer person designated, but also that you know how to do it yourself in case the light dimmer is not around (which happens in 35 per cent of all light dimmer designees).

Remember, anything that happens at the last minute to interrupt your concentration could throw you off-balance at the beginning of your talk. On the morning of the speech, avoid racing around and any unnecessary hectic activity.

Everything covered thus far should be customized for your own needs in the form of a checklist and multiple copies made and carried with you for individual speeches.

The evening before a speech is not the time to
engage in excessive hedonistic behavior.
Protect your brain from unnecessary abuse.

The investigator who also can give a good speech multiplies his or her effectiveness.

SIU 101: Kizorek/Finger

JUST BEFORE YOUR SPEECH

This is the time to build up your energy level. Walk around, introduce yourself to the individual members of the audience and tell them you are the speaker. Find out who they are. By now, you should know *why* they are at the speech, as well as have some sense of their values as a group. This knowledge will be critical to you during the speech itself. This is the audience who soon will be expecting you to stimulate, educate and solve problems. You, on the other hand, will want to move them to some type of action.

THE INTRODUCTION

Write your own introduction and give it to the person who will be speaking about you. Keep it short, unless absolutely necessary: avoid any type of lengthy chronology of your lifetime. The shorter the introduction, the better. The introductory person is not the speaker, you are.

As you take the podium or stand before the crowd, pause, smile and be natural. If you lead off with a humorous anecdote, have that story relate to the speech. The more appropriate the story, the more the audience will feel you are there to specifically address its needs and not play the comedian. Look around at the audience before you talk and open your speech with a flawless (because you have practiced) entry. The greatest likelihood of nervousness will be in this first minute of your presentation. Once the audience acknowledges that it likes you, especially with its laughter, you become empowered and energized.

What not to do: Do not boast, promote or advertise as you open your speech. Also, do not use trite phrases such as "I'm happy to be here," "thanks for inviting me." Get on with the presentation and dispense with the small talk.

THE BODY OF THE TALK

Because you have only a small note card and limited words, you will continue finding eye contact one of the easier techniques. As you continue your speech, keep in mind other successful procedures that will ensure your acceptance as a polished speaker:

- Pause frequently (and do not say *uhh*, *ah* and *uhm* before the pause).
- Slowly, scan the audience from one side to the other.

members of the audience walk out of the speech, many of them should be moved to act on your message.

If your presentation was mediocre, the crowd may leave lethargic. However, if you came across as poised, compelling, persuasive, inspirational, candid, convincing, passionate and caring, you may end up with an energized audience ready to carry on part of your mission for you.

Claimant Contact

This is one of the most delicate topics in the area of fraud investigations. One of the most broadly accepted rules of law is that if a claimant is represented by an attorney, the insurer, especially the claim department, is not allowed direct personal contact. At times, permission is granted by the claimant's attorney, although the attorneys like to be present when you talk to their clients.

Let us look at why claimant contact is proscribed. An attorney does not want you asking questions that will possibly compromise his or her client's claim or get his or her client into trouble. Therefore, you should not be contacting the claimant and talking about the claim. Then again, what else would you want to talk to the claimant about?

Consider the following situation. A claimant lives in a seven-story high-rise building and surveillance is to be conducted. No photographs of the claimant are available. Only a vague physical description is on file. Often certain means of claimant identification (Following the claimant from independent medical exams, scheduled therapy visits or deposition) are not available because of time constraints, uncooperative claimants who miss appointments, trial or settlement just around the corner. How do you identify that person?

This type of dilemma has been posed for almost every person who has worked bodily injury (BI) surveillances. It is critical to know who you are following, so many investigators use a mild personal contact pretext such as a floral delivery just to get a look at the face of the claimant. No questions are asked about the claim, employment, physical activities, hobbies or anything even remotely relating to the claim.

Can this technique lead to problems for the investigator? Perhaps, but not likely. An insurer, however, may be better off employing an independent

Claimant contact often is restricted
when an Attorney is involved.

vendor involved in this type of situation in order to maintain an arm's-length distance from the field investigation.

Here is an even better question: If you have a claimant who you are investigating for fraud and that person is not represented, do you have to warn the claimant of his or her rights concerning self-incrimination? One approach here is that you do not really know that the case may be fraudulent unless you talk to the claimant. Once a case is deemed prosecutable, it would be a good idea to follow more closely the rules relating to criminal prosecution.

Statement Taking

One of the greatest statement takers of the twentieth century is Hal Lipset, an insurance claims investigator and all-around, major-league detective. From the San Francisco headquarters of Lipset Services, Lipset has conducted tens of thousands of investigations – many of them involving statements. According to Lipset, "statement taking is a true art." He has retaken statements previously obtained by claims adjustors that, when finished, show the same witness recounting a story with the same facts but presented in such a way as to much better represent his own client's interests.

How does he do this? Lipset is a master at gathering information and doing it in such a way that the information gathered is organized and presented to support his client's position. "Two witnesses may see the same accident and have almost opposite recollections. Even a single witness may view the accident in opposite ways. I have interviewed what my client thought were hostile witnesses and the statements ended up favoring the position of the client," said Lipset.

Many of us have watched *Perry Mason* or *L.A. Law* and have heard the attorneys cry out, "your honor, counselor is leading the witness!" Can the investigator "lead the witness?" Lipset, who may be the only private eye in America who teaches a law school class on investigations, has his opinions.

An investigator cannot "lead" a witness by putting words in his or her mouth. The investigator can, however, help a witness refine his or her recollections. Investigators also can help a witness remember particulars that otherwise might have been forgotten. These investigative skills might be described or construed as "leading," but in reality, these techniques may more easily bring the witness to a true understanding of what he or she has perceived, according to Lipset.

homeowner fire claim. The SIU investigator will most likely have many other questions which will be determined and should be asked of the claimant during the course of each individual investigation. As always, the investigator should consult all company guidelines and policies regarding any type of statement taking prior to proceeding with an interview.

Prosecution

The majority of claimants are honest. Insurance fraud investigators should not be frustrated because only a small percentage of investigations reveal criminally fraudulent behavior or result in a prosecution. Keep in mind that the investigative efforts of special investigative unit personnel more often than not result in information showing that a claimant has exaggerated some portion of the claim. The savings in indemnity dollars by not paying out on a bogus claim may help to fund future fraud investigations.

Because there are many advantages of fraud convictions, not the least of which is a decrease in future bogus claims (as a result of publicity), close attention should be paid to the nuts and bolts of criminal prosecution.

According to the National Insurance Crime Bureau (NICB), four elements must be proven for a successful fraud prosecution. These elements include 1.) **the intent to defraud**, which indicates that the claimant both intentionally and deliberately deceived the insuring party. The individual must have had 2.) **knowledge** of the act of fraud and its potential consequences. It should be noted that individuals who have both intent and knowledge possibly will keep secret their past claims history and identities and also may falsely state or present the facts that have bearing on their claims.

Other elements necessary for successful prosecution include 3.) **misrepresentation**, in which a claimant creates an impression that his or her claim should be paid and also 4.) **reliance**, where without misrepresentation, the insurer would not in all probability have paid the claim to begin with.

After the groundwork is established by SIU staffers, any prosecutable cases should be brought to the attention of the NICB and/or the local state fraud bureau for review. Not all insurers are subscribers to the NICB, and company

Insurance fraud investigators should not be frustrated because of the small amount of prosecutions. Indemnity dollar savings are often a better barometer of SIU performance.

guidelines on referrals may vary, so a check of corporate policy is advised. Also, the NICB may be able to guide you on a specific investigation as well as alert you to a history of claims fraud by a specific claimant.

Although many states have created fraud bureaus and introduced legislation that toughens penalties for the commission of fraudulent activity relating to the insurance industry, the SIU investigator still may encounter difficulties when presenting his or her finished case to prosecutors. In some instances, prosecutors do not have experience in handling insurance fraud prosecutions or are reluctant to get involved because of the comparatively low dollar figures involved.

To better the odds of getting a case accepted for possible criminal prosecution, the SIU investigator must not only have the case packaged with no stones left unturned but also should take the long-term approach of training local prosecutors to recognize the severity of insurance fraud and the need for punishment of those who abuse the system. When bringing their cases to the attention of prosecutors, investigators can provide articles and examples of similar situations that were successfully adjudicated in other jurisdictions.

The following guidelines for investigation can be helpful to even senior SIU staffers.

Investigation Guidelines

This chapter contains very specific avenues of investigation for a variety of suspected fraud investigations. These lists have been created, for the most part, by veteran fraud investigator Gary M. Schild. Schild has been a senior SIU investigator for two major insurers and created these lists for the investigators he trained.

These lists are *so* thorough that you will find it impractical to apply each avenue of investigation to every potential fraud case. However, if an investigator is intensely pursuing an important case the step-by-step suggestions will be invaluable to guarantee a "no stones left unturned" strategy.

At the end of the chapter are sample forms investigators should use to *legally* gain access to certain types of information. As with any type of investigation, investigators should understand and follow insurance-company policies, guidelines and procedures during all investigative efforts. Individual SIU units may have specific documents for the release of claimant information, which should be used whenever possible by SIU staffers.

Auto Theft Investigations in Suspicious Claims

The following guidelines should be referenced during an auto theft investigation to ensure thoroughness. The SIU investigator always should explore any other avenue of investigation that may be pertinent to the case. Specific SIU policies should be consulted prior to any investigation. If evidence of fraud has developed, submit claim to the NICB or state fraud bureau where applicable.

1. **Confer with the Claim Representative.**

   A. Review the recorded statement of the insured if taken by a claim representative.

   B. Check for other claims involving the same vehicle.

   C. Make sure the claim representative reported to the NICB.

   D. If the vehicle is recovered, get the details of recovery and current location of the car.

2. **Contact the Lienholder of the Car.**

   A. What is the current balance of the loan?

   B. When was the loan taken out?

   C. What are the monthly payments?

   D. Is the insured up-to-date on payments?

   E. Was the car repossessed?

   F. Any recent contact with the insured?

3. **Contact the Insurance Agent.**

   A. Any recent contact with the insured? Did the insured call to confirm or change coverage?

   B. Does the agent have any information on the insured's financial condition?

   C. When was the policy first written?

   D. Prior carrier?

   E. Did the agent ever personally inspect the car?

   F. Photographs available?

4. **Contact the Appraiser If the Car Was Recovered and Inspected.**

   A. Was there evidence of forcible entry to the vehicle?

   B. Was the ignition system forcibly defeated?

   C. Any indication of overkill? (Unnecessary vandalism intended to total the vehicle).

   D. Is there evidence of the surgical removal of parts or the radio/stereo system?

   E. Is the vehicle burned? If so, is cause-and-origin (C&O) investigation needed?

   F. Was the vehicle stripped prior to being burned?

   G Any indication of mechanical troubles? (Claimant possibly filed false theft report in order to have mechanical problems covered by insurance).

   H. May need to obtain oil and transmission samples or have mechanic examine vehicle for possible prior mechanical difficulties.

   I. Any fresh collision damage on the vehicle? (Claimant possibly filed false theft report in order to escape responsibility for hit and run or other unreported accident.)

5. **Inspect the Car If Recovered**

   A. Photograph and inspect the car. Get the mileage.

   B. Check the interior of the car for repair invoices, registration papers, insurance papers, etc.

   C. If there is doubt as to whether the steering column is really defeated or not, you may need to use an expert to examine the steering column.

   D. Inspect VIN plate and verify legitimacy of VIN number.

6. **Interview the Insured.** (For a sample question format, review "Question Format for Vehicle Theft Interview," at the end of this segment.)

   A. Make sure vehicle was legally parked and not in police impound lot.

   B. Inspect paperwork on vehicle including the title, registration, repair bills, purchase invoice, parts invoices of items added to vehicle, etc.

   C. If a cellular telephone was present in the vehicle, get itemized telephone records.

   D. If the policy is new or the identity of the insured is in doubt, obtain as much identification as possible (Social Security card, driver's license, etc.)

   E. If there appears to be a financial motive involved in the theft of the vehicle, question the insured concerning his overall finances. Also, obtain a release in order to run the insured's credit history.

7. **Verify the Alibi of the Insured.**

8. **Run a License Plate on the Vehicle. Does It Issue to the Insured and to the Insured's Vehicle?**

9. **Check the Repair History of the Car with Repair Shops.**

10. **Run a Title History (Optional) – Necessary If a Policy Is New Or If You Suspect a "Paper Car."**

11. **Obtain the Police Reports. Speak with the Investigator, If One Is Assigned.**

12. **Report the Theft to the NICB and Check the Vehicle Through Any Available Databases.**

13. **Canvass the Area Where the Car Allegedly Was Stolen and Where It Was Recovered (Optional).**

14. **Follow Up on Any Hits Received Through Database Check.**

15. **Verify the Claimant's Address. Is He Or She a Rate Evader?**

16. **If evidence of fraud has been developed submit claim to NICB or state fraud bureau when applicable.**

Question Format for Vehicle Theft Interview

SIU investigators who wish to take a recorded or written statement of an insured making a claim after an alleged vehicle theft should be well-prepared in advance of the interview period. The following list should aid in the investigator's preparation, but as in any segment of an investigation, company guidelines and policies regarding statement taking and claimant contact should be consulted prior to the interview.

A. **OPENING:**

This is _____YOUR NAME_____ interviewing _____PERSON YOU ARE INTERVIEWING_____.

Today is _____DATE_____.

Today's interview is being conducted at _____LOCATION_____.

B. Please state your full name. Are you married? If so, what is your spouse's name and maiden name?

C. Do I have your permission to record this statement?

D. What is your Social Security number? What is your driver's license number?

E. What is your address?

F. How long have you lived there? (If the answer is under two years, follow up with next question.)

G. What was your previous address?

H. What is your date of birth? (You may want the county of birth as well.)

I. Are you employed and by whom? (Get the details, as well as the name of a supervisor.)

J.   How long have you been employed at this location? (If less than one year, ask about previous employment.)

K.   Do you have any other insurance on the stolen vehicle? If yes, obtain all the details.

L.   Is this the first time you have had a vehicle stolen? If there are prior thefts, obtain all the details.

M.   Obtain the following details on the stolen vehicle:
   1. Make and model of vehicle
   2. Type of vehicle
   3. Year of vehicle
   4. Vehicle identifican number (VIN)
   5. License plate number
   6. Special features on this vehicle?
      a. Upgraded stereo
      b. Alarm
      c. Paint job, etc.

N.   When and where was the vehicle bought? For how much and how was it paid for?

O.   Where is a copy of the invoice?

P.   Who is the lien holder on the vehicle, including the loan number and telephone number?

Q.   What were the monthly payments, the terms of the loan, the length and amount financed? Were you up-to-date on your payments? If not, get the details of why and how far behind.

R.   Where was this vehicle usually parked?

S.   Who has permission to drive this vehicle?

T.   Who has keys to the vehicle and how many sets are there? Are any missing?

U.   Are you sure that no one with access to the vehicle has taken or borrowed it?

V.   How long have you been insured with your present carrier? Previous insurer?

W.   Has the vehicle been involved in any accidents? Where and when?

X.   Where were the repairs from previous accidents made?

Y.   Were the accidents reported to any insurance company?

Z.   What was the mechanical condition of the vehicle just before the theft? If recent work was done, where and when? Invoices? (Ask the claimant to provide invoices.)

AA. Was there any body damage on the vehicle stolen? What was the condition of the exterior?

BB. What was the condition of the interior of the vehicle the day of the theft? Was there any personal property in the vehicle at the time of the theft?

CC. What was the odometer reading on the vehicle when it was stolen?

DD. When was the last time the vehicle was driven and where was it driven? (If the interviewee drove it, was anyone with?)

EE. When was the last time the vehicle was seen? Was it locked, legally parked or were the keys left inside? Any hidden keys?

FF. Was the vehicle for sale around the period it was stolen? If yes, how much were you asking? Any prospective buyers?

GG. Did the vehicle have an alarm? Was the alarm on? Type of alert – horn, lights, siren?

HH. When did the insured become aware that the vehicle was missing? How was he or she notified?

II. Where was the insured between the last time the vehicle was seen and when it was discovered missing? Who was with him or her during this time? Get as detailed as you can.

JJ. When the theft was discovered, did the claimant observe any sign of forcible entry? If the claimant needed a ride home after the theft, who did so?

KK. How was the police report made? Police notified as soon as possible? If not, why not? Which department? Any detective assigned?

LL. Are there any possible witnesses, such as neighbors?

MM. When did the insured notify your agent of the theft? If there was a delay in reporting, probe.

NN. Has the insured's vehicle been recovered? If yes, when and by whom? Where is the vehicle now and in what condition?

OO. Are there any persons the insured might have suspected in the theft?

PP. In closing, ask the insured to restate:
1. Full name;
2. Social Security number and date of birth; and
3. Ask one more time if permission has been granted for this statement to be recorded.

(If this is a signed statement, have the interviewee sign and date the last page, *as well as* initial the bottom of each page and any changes within the body of the statement.)

Personal Injury Investigations

The following guidelines should be referred to when pursuing (non-auto) personal- injury investigations. The investigation will focus for the most part on two areas, determining the extent of liability while also confirming the identity of and actual loss suffered by the claimant. Always consult company policies before proceeding with any type of investigation.

1. **Confer with the Claim Representative.**

   A. What investigation has been done to this point? Is there additional investigation to do regarding the liability investigation?

   B. Liability investigation will focus on how the person was injured. Did anyone hear or see the person fall? Were there any hazards present? Was the insured notified of the hazard? If so, had the insured taken steps to correct it?

   C. Did the claimant do anything to contribute to his or her injury (for example, was the claimant careless, intoxicated, etc.?)

   D. Is the identity of the claimant in doubt?

   E. Any response from the Index Bureau?

   F. Check the computer system for other claims. Do not neglect to check any in-house databases.

2. **Conduct an On-Scene Investigation.**

   A. Pursue whatever logical investigative steps that have not yet been pursued by the claim representative's investigation.

   B. Photograph the area where the accident occurred.

C. Canvass the area of accident for possible witnesses where appropriate.

D. Interview any witnesses. Determine if they have any type of relationship with or to the claimant or insured.

3. **Index Bureau.**

    A. Contact the insurance carriers involved on any index hits. Get the details of these claims.

    B. Index the claimant under any aliases or maiden names.

    C. Re-index the claimant before settling, if the claim is suspicious.

4. **Interview the Claimant.**

    A. If represented by an attorney, interview the claimant in the presence of that attorney.

    B. Obtain the details of the incident.

    C. Get the name, address and the phone of any witnesses, also their relationships to the claimant.

    D. Have the claimant sign any releases needed for further investigation (see the release forms at the end of this chapter).

    E. Obtain identification from the claimant: driver's license, Social Security card, etc.

    F. If the identity of the claimant is in doubt, press him or her for background information such as date of birth, county and hospital where born, Social Security number and what state it was issued in, prior employers, prior addresses, marital status, children's names, where and when they were born, etc.

5. **Verify the Identity of the Claimant**

    A. Check the Social Security number through the appropriate sources.

    B. Do a driver's license check (if necessary).

    C. Pull a copy of the claimant's birth certificate (if necessary).

    D. Does the information that the claimant provided concerning any prior addresses and employers check out?

E. Do a courthouse check. Look for other claims involving the claimant.

F. Do a courthouse criminal check. Does an arrest sheet show an alias for the claimant?

G. Neighborhood canvass may provide useful information, but extreme care must be taken to avoid accusations of slander.

6. **Verify All Specials.**

A. Check the wage loss in person. Does the company exist? Is the company a mail drop or answering service? Any on-the-job injuries or worker's compensation claims?

B. Verify the medical bills: Is the doctor licensed? (Check with the state licensing board.)

C. Check the clinic in person if at all possible. Is the equipment indicated in the physicians bill present on the premises? If the investigator has a signed medical release from the claimant, inspect the entire file including physician notes and sign-in logs.

D. If a medical release has been obtained, attempt to get the health insurance records from the claimant's employer. (These records may often reveal a pre-existing condition that the claimant is attempting to conceal).

7. **If Any Evidence of Fraud has Developed, Submit the Claim to the NICB or State Fraud Bureau Where Applicable.**

Insured involvement should be investigated in suspicious burglary claims.

Burglary Investigation

Investigating burglary claims involve several steps. Both the agent and the claim representative can provide information relevant to the claim, and should be contacted as a matter of course. Before investigating a burglary claim, insurance company policies should be thoroughly reviewed. Any suspicious claim should be referred to NICB or if appropriate, state fraud bureau.

1. **Contact the Insurance Agent for Background Information.**

   A. How long has coverage been in place?

   B. Prior carrier?

   C. Any change in coverage recently? Any recent calls confirming coverage?

   D. Financial condition of the insured?

   E. Any recent changes in the insured's life? (divorce, loss of job, etc.)

2. **Confer with the Claim Representative.**

   A. What investigation has been done to this point?

   B. Has claim been submitted to PILR (Property Insurance Loss Register) and your local loss bureau?

   C. If any hits received from PILR or your local loss bureau, contact the companies involved to see if any duplication on claim.

   D. Check computer system for other losses. Also check any in-house computer databases.

   E. Has the claim representative noted any unusual aspects of the claim?

3. **Pick Up a Copy of the Police Report and Interview the Investigator If One is Assigned.**

   A. Are there any discrepancies between the items listed on the police report and those on the proof of loss?

   B. Any suspects developed?

   C. Any forced entry?

   D. Any property recovered?

   E. Investigator aware of any prior theft or burglary reports by this insured?

   F. Has the insured been cooperative with the police?

4. **Review the Receipts Submitted by the Insured.**

   A. Insist that the insured submits original receipts, not photocopies.

   B. Look for evidence of whiteout, alterations, improper sales tax, out-of-sequence numbers, etc.

   C. Verify the receipts with the store (in person, if possible). Make sure the goods were not returned, exchanged or brought back for service.

   D. If there are database hits, review prior claim files to determine if the same receipts were submitted.

5. **Interview the Insured and Inspect Loss Location.**

   A. Is the point of entry believable?

   B. Was there an alarm on the premises? Was the alarm activated? If not, why not?

   C. Are the contents claimed consistent with the lifestyle?

   D. Is the insured claiming unusual items stolen? (For example, shoes, clothes, ironing board, lamps, etc.)

   E. Was the family dog present during the break-in? If not, why not?

   F. Does the scene match the insured's story (For example: Is the carpet matted down where the console TV once was?)

   G. Question the insured and the family as to their whereabouts and verify their alibis.

H. Question the insured regarding each missing item; where and when purchased, description of the item and how purchased.

I. Question the insured regarding the loss history, prior insurance carriers, prior addresses, etc.

J. If the insured's identity is in doubt, insist on an ID: Social Security card, driver's license, etc.

K. Question the insured regarding their finances, obtain a release so a credit history can be run.

6. Canvass the Neighborhood.

A. This is only done in select cases and should be done shortly after the loss date.

B. Interview of the landlord may yield useful information.

C. Were the neighbors aware of the contents in the insured location prior to the loss?

D. If recently divorced, interview spouse. It could be beneficial if items such as furniture are being claimed.

E. Did neighbors see insured moving any items out prior to burglary?

F. What activity did neighbors observe around property on date of loss?

7. Exam under Oath (EUO).

A. It may be appropriate to compel the insured to submit to an exam under oath (EUO) if further investigation is called for. A demand for itemized telephone records for the claimant's residence can often prove useful.

8. If Evidence of Fraud has been Developed Submit Claim to NICB or State Fraud Bureau Where Applicable.

Automobile Accidents: Injury

Investigation of automobile accidents with injury can be complex. Claimants as well as vehicles must be researched for possible prior claims and relationships of those involved should be checked into. Please consult company policies and guidelines before proceeding with this type of investigation. If evidence of fraud is gathered, referral of the case to the NICB or appropriate state fraud bureau should be completed.

1. **Confer with the Claim Representative.**

    A. Compile the details of the accident.

    B. Check the databases for any prior losses.

    C. Check the plates on both the claimant and the insured cars.

    D. Check the computer system for other losses involving the claimant and/or the insured. Also check all available in-house databases.

    E. Check all Social Security numbers obtained through credit database sources.

2. **Confer with the Appraiser.**

    A. Is the damage older than the date of loss? (Excessive rust, fading, etc.?) The investigator may be able to confirm old damage through checking accident reports, contacting other insurance carriers, repair shops or even a neighborhood canvass.

    B. Is the damage consistent with the facts of the accident?

    C. Obtain photographs, if taken. Even photographs of little or no damage may be of use in cases with built-up medicals.

D. Consider using an accident-reconstruction expert if the appraiser indicates that it does not appear that the cars impacted each other. (Possible paper-accident.)

3. **Confer with the Insurance Agent.**

   A. When was coverage obtained?

   B. Any recent changes in coverage?

   C. Prior carrier?

   D. Did the agent ever see or inspect the insured car?

4. **Interview the Insured.**

   A. Get the details of the accident.

   B. Discuss other claims or accidents that the insured may have had.

   C. Does the insured know the people in the other car? Family relationships? Friends?

   D. Inspect the paperwork on the car.

   E. Where was the car repaired?

   F. Get the details on the medical treatments and the wage loss being claimed.

   G. Obtain releases.

5. **Interview the Claimants.**

   A. Get the details of the accident.

   B. Discuss other claims or accidents that the claimants may have had.

   C. Do the claimants know the insured? If so, in what capacity?

   D. Name of the insurance carrier for the claimant car?

   E. Get the details of the medical treatment and the wage loss claimed.

   F. Obtain releases.

   G. If the identity of the claimants is in doubt, obtain as much indentification as possible. (Social Security number, drivers license, etc.)

6. **Follow Up on Any Index Hits Received.**

Staged accidents are __not__ entertaining.

7. **Run a Database Check on All Cars Involved To See If There Were Any *Other* Accidents.**

8. **Interview Witnesses. Determine any Connections to the Insured or the Claimant.**

9. **Run a Title History on All Cars.**

10. **Obtain Police Report. Interview Officer Who Responded to the Scene.**

11. **Inspect the Accident Scene and Canvass for Additional Witnesses.**

12. **Check the License Plates on all the Vehicles Involved in the Accident.**

13. **Verify Specials.**

    A. Check medical bills in person, with a release in order to obtain the entire file including physician's notes and sign-in logs. Is the equipment described in medical invoices present at the clinic location?

    B. Check the wage loss in person. Does the company exist?

    C. If it appears that medicals are inflated, an independent analysis of those bills may be in order.

14. **Courthouse Check May Reveal Other Claims or Accidents.**

15. **If Case Lingers, Re-index the Claimant Every 3 - 6 Months.**

16. **If Evidence of Fraud has been Developed Submit the Claim to NICB or a State Fraud Bureau Where Applicable.**

Automobile Accidents: Collision

When investigating automobile collision claims, computer databases can be very helpful in determining involvement in other accidents, ownership of the vehicle and confirming claimant information. The SIU investigator should consult the insurance company's policy manual before proceeding with any type of investigation. If evidence of fraud is gathered, refer the claim to the NICB or state fraud bureau where appropriate.

1. **Confer with the Claim Representative.**

    A. Obtain the details of the accident.

    B. Check the computer databases for any hits.

    C. Check the license plate. Does it issue to the insured?

    D. Check the computer system for other losses. Check any in-house databases that are available.

2. **Confer With the Appraiser.**

    A. Is the damage older than the date of loss?

    B. Is there damage unrelated to this accident?

    C. Is the damage consistent with the facts of the accident?

    D. Obtain a photograph of the car (if one was taken).

3. **Confer With the Insurance Agent.**

    A. When was coverage obtained?

    B. Any recent changes on the coverage?

    C. Prior carrier?

    D. Did the agent ever see or inspect the insured vehicle?

Most collision claims are unquestionably compensable.
Some are questionably noncompensable.

4. **Interview the Insured.**

    A. Obtain the details of the accident.

    B. Discuss prior claims and insurance carriers.

    C. Where was the car normally parked?

    D. Where was the car repaired?

    E. View any paperwork on the car registration, title, repair invoices.

5. **Run a Title History If Ownership Is in Doubt or if the Vehicle was Acquired Shortly Before the Loss Date. An Interview of the Prior Owner May Reveal Damage Existed Prior to the Loss Date.**

6. **Interview the Neighbors, the Repair Shop Or Anyone Who May Have Seen the Car Prior to the Date of Loss. Can They Tell You If Collision Damage Existed Prior to the Date of Loss? Photograph Is Helpful When Canvassing.**

7. **If New Business, Contact Prior Insurance Carrier To See if Damage Existed Before the Date of the Loss.**

8. **If Any Hits From a Computer Database, Follow Up with the Insurance Carrier Involved. Is There any Indication of Multiple Policies Taken Out on the Vehicle Just Prior to the Loss Date?**

9. **Obtain the Police Report. Check with the Police for any Other Reports on File Involving the Insured or Their Vehicle.**

10. **Interview Other Driver Involved: Any Indication of Collusion Between the Two Drivers?**

11. **Consider Accident Reconstructionist If Indications Are That You Are Dealing with a Paper Accident.**

12. **If Evidence of Fraud has been Developed Submit the Claim to a State Fraud Bureau Where Applicable.**

Arson Investigation

The investigator who is looking into a potential arson will be dealing with numerous individuals including fire-department and law-enforcement personnel, cause-and-origin (C&O) investigators and, of course, the general public. Great care should be taken when gathering facts in any investigation and a thorough knowledge of laws and policies is recommended before proceeding. If evidence of fraud is gathered, report the claim to the NICB, or the state fraud bureau where applicable and also the State Fire Marshall's office.

1. **Confer with the Claim Representative.**

    A. Has a C&O investigator been retained? If so, what are his or her initial findings?

    B. What additional investigation has the C&O investigator been instructed to do? Coordinate each other's efforts, do not duplicate.

    C. Check the computer system for other losses. Also, check any available in-house databases.

    D. Has the claim been submitted to the Property Insurance Loss Register (PILR) and your local loss bureau? If there are any hits, get the details from other insurance companies.

2. **Contact the C&O Investigator.**

    A. Were pets away from the residence at the time of the fire?

    B. Was the fire intentionally set? How did the investigator arrive at that conclusion? Were significant items missing from the home (For example, appliances, furniture, etc.) or were personal or sentimental items removed prior to the fire?

    C. Was there forced entry to the building?

    D. What have police and fire officials done?

E. Have the C&O investigator interview the firemen initially responding. What did they see? Was the building secure?

F. Who reported the fire? The reporting individual should be interviewed.

G. Status of burglary and fire alarms? If applicable, obtain alarm company's records.

H. Have the C&O investigator obtain all pertinent fire reports.

I. Any subrogation potential? (For example, faulty coffee maker.)

J. Is the Fire Department making the same C&O determination as the insurance company expert?

3. **Contact the Insurance Agent for Background Information.**

A. How long insured?

B. Prior carrier?

C. Any recent contact with the insured?

D. Did the insured call recently to verify coverage, up policy amounts or make any changes?

E. Does the agent have any information on the financial condition of the insured?

F. Are there any recent changes in the insured's life? (For example, divorce, loss of job, etc.)

4. **Obtain a Copy of the Police Report and Interview the Investigator (if one was assigned).**

A. Any suspects listed?

B. Does the insured's alibi check out?

C. Does the investigator have any background information on the insured?

D. Get the details of the police investigation, what the police have done and what they intend to do.

5. **Obtain a Recorded Statement from the Insured (See Next Chapter: "Question Format for Homeowner Fire Investigation Interview").**

6. **Interview Any Witnesses, Determining Their Relationship to the Insured.**

7. **Interview Anyone Else Who May Have Knowledge of the Incident (For Example, Neighbors, Employees, Family Members, Business Competitors, etc.)**

8. **Get a Signed Release From the Insured to Pursue the Financial Background and On-scene Investigation.**

9. **Verify the insured's alibi.**

10. **Do a Background and Financial Investigation on the Insured.**

    A. *Do a courthouse check. Check for litigation, civil and criminal history involving the insured. Bankruptcy filings by the insured?

    B. *Do a courthouse check on the insured property. Look for mortgages, liens, taxes paid, owner of property, etc.

    C. Interview the associates, customers and vendors who do business with the insured.

    D. Run a credit history on the insured, if a release has been obtained.

    E. Obtain IRS reports for the past two years of the insured (release needed).

    F. Obtain business records if it is a commercial loss. Interview suppliers and customers.

    G. Obtain itemized telephone records from the insured's location, also car telephone records.

    * Note: Both "A" and "B" can be done by a private investigation firm or asset searching firm.

11. **A Neighborhood Canvass in the Area of the Fire May Prove Helpful. Any Activity observed on the Night of Fire? Was the Insured Observed Removing Contents Prior to the Fire?**

12. **Verify receipts or information provided in support of the contents portion of the claim.**

13. **Exam Under Oath (EUO): an Option if It Appears That There Is Insured Involvement.**

14. **Monitor Police and Fire Marshal's Investigation for Any Possible Results.**

Question Format for Homeowner Fire Investigation Interview

SIU staffers who wish to take a recorded statement of an insured making a claim after a fire in or on the property of their home should be well-prepared in advance of the interview period. The following list should aid in the investigator's preparation, but as in any segment of an investigation, company guidelines and policies regarding statement taking and claimant contact should be consulted prior to the interview.

This is _____YOUR NAME_____ interviewing Mr. or Mrs. _____WITNESS_____ _____NAME_____ concerning the fire at _____LOCATION OF LOSS_____ that occurred on _____DATE OF LOSS_____ at approximately _____TIME OF LOSS_____ am/pm.

Today's date is _____DATE OF INTERVIEW_____ and this interview is being conducted at _____LOCATION OF INTERVIEW_____.

A. Please state your full name.

B. What is your Social Security number?

C. What is your date of birth?

D. Are you aware this interview is being tape recorded?

E. Did you give your permission for this interview to be tape recorded?

F. Where were you residing at the time of the fire?

G. Where are you residing now? (Obtain the address and telephone number).

H.   Who was residing at the insured location at the time of the fire?

I.   Do we have your permission to enter upon your property for the purpose of investigating the cause of the fire?

J.   Do we have your permission to remove any item(s) that may lead us to the cause and origin of this fire?

K.   If necessary, do we have your permission to return to your property at a later date to collect evidence from the fire?

Note: The typical personal lines homeowners policy usually gives the insurance company the right to perform the actions described in questions I, J, and K. However, take nothing for granted and review the policy which applies to the claim under investigation.

L.   What is your marital status?

M.   Have you had any prior marriages?

N.   Do you have any financial obligations from those prior marriages?

O.   What is your current spouse's name?

P.   Are there any divorce proceedings underway regarding you and your spouse?

Q.   What other names have you gone by in your lifetime? Please include maiden names, previously married names and aliases or nicknames.

R.   What is your occupation?

S.   Who are you employed by?

T.   What is the address and telephone number of your employer?

U.   What is the name of your immediate supervisor?

V.   What is your spouse's occupation?

W.   Who is your spouse's employer?

X.   What is the address and telephone number of your spouse's employer?

Y.   Who is your spouse's immediate supervisor?

Z. Do you have any children? What are your children's names and ages?

AA. Do your children reside with you at the insured location?

BB. What pets are kept at the insured location?

CC. Were the pets in the house at the time of the fire?

DD. If not, why were they missing from the house?

EE. Is any type of business being run out of the insured location? (If so, obtain details).

FF. Do you own any property other than the insured location? (If so, obtain details).

GG. Is there any other insurance on the insured location or its contents?

HH. Has there been any recent remodeling on the insured location? If so, obtain the names of the contractors involved, and where the building materials were purchased.

II. What was the condition of the structure before the fire?

JJ. Were any repairs needed?

KK. Any problems with bug or termite infestation?

LL. Are there any building, health or zoning violations against the property?

MM. Have you had any recent appraisals on the property?

NN. Who did the appraisal? Why was the appraisal done? What were the results of the appraisal?

OO. Has this property ever been offered for sale? (If so, obtain details).

PP. Have you ever suffered loss by fire or theft in your lifetime?

QQ. Have you ever filed an insurance claim other than a health insurance claim?

RR. Provide details of any insurance claims you have filed including: date, type and location of the occurrence, location of occurrence, the insurance company involved and the amount of any settlement.

SS. Have you or your spouse ever been arrested? (If so, obtain details).

TT. Have you or your spouse ever filed for bankruptcy? (If so, obtain details).

UU. Have you ever been a party to a civil suit?

VV. Has a judgment ever been entered against you in a civil suit?

WW. Please provide details concerning any civil suit that you have been a party to.

XX. When did you purchase the insured location? Who did you buy it from?

YY. How long has the loss location been insured with
_____NAME OF PRESENT INSURANCE COMPANY_____?

ZZ. Has this location ever been insured with another insurance company? (If so, obtain details).

a. Have you filed any other insurance claim relating to this property or its contents? (If so, obtain details).

b. Has there ever been a fire at a location that you were living at or had a financial interest in? (If so, obtain details).

c. How long have you lived at the loss location?

d. Please provide addresses you have lived at or had a financial interest in going back 10 years.

e. Are you the sole owner of the insured location?

f. If anyone else has a financial interest in the loss location, please provide their name, address, telephone and describe their financial stake in the insured property.

g. What was the price paid for the loss location?

h. How much was the down payment?

i. Where did you obtain the down payment?

j. What was the amount of your loan at the time of purchase?

k.   What were the terms of your loan? Interest rate? Length of note? Balloon payment due? Monthly payments? Any special loan provisions? etc.

l.   What financial institution financed the purchase?

m.   What is the current balance on your loan?

n.   Are you up to date on your payments?

o.   Has your lender ever started foreclosure proceedings against you in regards to this property?

p.   What are the property taxes on the loss location?

q.   Are your property taxes paid up to date?

r.   Have there been any special assessments leveled against the insured property? (If so, obtain details).

s.   Are there any other mortgages or liens on the insured property? (If so, obtain details).

t.   Are there any liens on any of your personal property? (If so, obtain details).

u.   Is any of your personal property being financed? (If so, obtain details).

v.   Have you ever had any personal property or real estate repossessed? (If so, obtain details).

w.   Do you have a financial interest in any business?

x.   What is your monthly take home pay?

y.   What is your spouses monthly take home pay?

z.   Do you have any other sources of income? (For example, stocks, bonds, inheritance, other real estate, interest income, etc.).

aa.   What other assets do you have? (Obtain details).

bb.   Where are your checking and savings accounts?

cc.   What was the balance of these accounts at the time of the fire?

dd. Do you have any outstanding loans other than the loan on your home? (If so, give details).

ee. Are you current on all your loan payments?

ff. Please provide the name, address and telephone numbers of these lending institutions.

gg. What charge cards do you have?

hh. What is the balance on your charge cards?

ii. Are you up to date on your payments?

jj. What are your monthly utility expenses? (Electric, gas, water, sewer, garbage pickup).

kk. Do you have any other financial obligations? (For example, alimony, child support, supporting an elderly parent, etc.)

ll. How would you assess your financial condition at the time of the fire?

mm. Was any personal property moved out of the insured location prior to the fire? If so, why was it moved and where was it moved to?

nn. Are you leasing storage space from anyone?

oo. Did any personal items such as family photos, mementos, financial records, survive the fire? If so, how did these items escape damage?

pp. Where is your copy of your insurance policy? Was it destroyed or damaged by smoke? If not, why not?

qq. Ask the insured to describe the contents of each room and where the contents were located within the room.

rr. For major items such as furniture, appliances, television, stereo, ask the insured to state the brand name, where and when purchased, price paid, etc.

ss. Do you have any photos of the interior of your home taken before the fire that would help to document the existence and condition of your personal property?

tt. Have you had any recent problems with your furnace or air-conditioning system? If so, obtain details as to what the problem was and who repaired it.

uu. Any recent problems with your electrical system? If so, what was the nature of problem and who repaired it?

vv. Have there been any problems with any of the electric or gas powered appliances in your home? If so, what was the nature of the problem and the name of the repairman who fixed it?

ww. How many entrances are there to your house?

xx. What types of locks are on each door?

yy. What types of locks are on the windows?

zz. Do all the windows have screen/storm windows?

Aa. Have you changed any of the locks since you have lived in the house? (If yes, ask next question).

Bb. When were the locks changed? Why were they changed? Who did the work?

Cc. At the time of the fire, who had keys to the house?

Dd. Have any keys to the house ever been lost or stolen?

Ee. Are all keys accounted for since the fire?

Ff. Who was the last person to leave the house before the fire? (If that person is not insured, locate him or her and set up an interview).

Gg. What time did you leave the house? Did anyone see you?

Hh. Who else was with you?

Ii. What door did you exit the residence through?

Jj. Did you lock all the doors and windows before leaving?

Kk. Did you leave any lights on?

Ll. Had you been using any appliances before leaving?

Mm. Were any appliances turned on when you left?

Nn. Were you or any other occupants smoking before leaving the house? If so, in what room did the smoking take place?

Oo. Are there any accelerants kept in the house?

Pp. Describe the exact location of any accelerants kept in the house and give the reason they are stored in the house.

Qq. Were all the utilities (gas, water, electric) on in the house when you left?

Rr. Is the house equipped with a burglar or smoke alarm? Please describe the type of alarm. Was the alarm activated when you left?

Ss. Were any visitors at your house the day of the fire or the day before? Who were they and what was the reason for their visit?

Tt. Did anyone see you leave the house?

Uu. Do you have a telephone in your house? Do you have a cellular or car telephone? (Attempt to obtain all itemized telephone records).

Vv. After you left the house, where did you go?

Ww. If you drove away from the insured location give a description of the vehicle you were in.

Xx. Describe the clothing you were wearing and give a physical and clothing description of anyone who was with you.

Yy. Describe your movements from the time you left your residence until the time you learned of the fire. Describe where you went, who you saw, what you did, what telephone calls you made and why, etc. (Obtain as many details as possible!)

Zz. Did you return to your residence before the fire was discovered? What was the reason for your return?

A1. How did you learn of the fire?

B1. Where were you when you heard about the fire?

C1. When did you return to your home?

D1. Who was there at that time?

E1. Did you speak with police and fire officials?

F1. Do the authorities have a suspect in mind or in custody? Did the firemen say how they gained entrance to the residence?

G1. What did they tell you concerning where and how the fire started?

H1. Did they tell you how entry was gained to the house?

I1. After examining the home, do you have an opinion as to how entry was gained or where and how the fire started? What do you base that opinion on?

J1. Did it appear that any contents were missing from your home?

K1. Did you remove any contents after the fire? If so, where are these contents now?

L1. Have you spoken with your neighbors? Did they notice any suspicious activity?

M1. Do you know who called the Fire Department?

N1. Is there anyone that you suspect of starting the fire?

O1. Is anyone harboring a grudge against you or anyone in your family?

P1. Do you have any knowledge who is responsible for setting this fire?

Q1. Did you set the fire yourself?

R1. Do you plan to rebuild the insured location?

S1. What steps have you taken since the fire to preserve and protect the insured location?

T1. Can you think of anything else that might assist us in our investigation?

U1. Do you wish to change any of the answers you have given to my questions?

V1. Have you understood all of my questions?

W1. Is there anything else you would like to add to this statement?

X1. Have all of your answers been truthful?

Y1. Would you please restate your full name?

Z1. Would you please restate your Social Security number?

A2. Would you please restate your date of birth?

B2. Have you been aware that this interview was tape recorded?

C2. Did you give your permission for that recording to take place?

D2. Thank you!

Releases

During the course of insurance investigations it is sometimes necessary to secure a release or waiver to obtain information and records from individuals involved in the investigation. Following are several generic release forms that may be used during the course of the investigation. It should be noted that individual insurance company guidelines, policies and all laws pertaining to the release of information should be reviewed prior to using these forms. Also, individual insurance companies may have specific release forms that should be used during the investigator's efforts.

Insurance Company

Address

Logo, here

AUTHORIZATION: RELEASE OF BIRTH RECORDS

I, _____ , DO HEREBY

AUTHORIZE _____

AND THE _____

INSURANCE COMPANY TO OBTAIN COPIES OF MY BIRTH CERTIFICATE

AS WELL AS THE BIRTH CERTIFICATES OF MY CHILDREN.

Signature: _____ Date:_____

Witness: _____ Date:_____

MEDICAL INFORMATION CONSENT FORM: Read Carefully

CLAIM NUMBER	INSURED/CLIENT	DATE OF ACCIDENT

PATIENT'S NAME	DATE OF BIRTH	PATIENT'S ADDRESS

NAME(S) AND/OR CLASSES OF MEDICAL PROVIDER(S) AUTHORIZED TO RELEASE MEDICAL INFORMATION:

TYPE OF INFORMATION OR SPECIFIC MEDICAL RECORDS AND DATE(S) OF TREATMENT TO BE RELEASED.

RESTRICTIONS:

This authorization (or a copy thereof) will allow the person(s) listed above to furnish _____ _____ and its legal representatives specific medical information for treatment and diagnosis related to injuries, sickness or disease sustained by the patient and arising out of or related to this accident or medical condition.

This information will be used only to establish the merit of claims for benefits or damages presented to the insurance company.

This information will not be released to other persons without your permission, except to protect you, ourselves or in compliance with any applicable law, governmental regulation or court order.

For your protection, the information is not directly available to you. With your consent, it may be provided to your physician or legal representative.

This authorization can be revoked at any time. It is not valid for more than one year.

I HAVE READ THE ABOVE AND UNDERSTAND THE PURPOSE AND USE OF THIS MEDICAL INFORMATION RELEASE AUTHORIZATION.

_____   _____
SIGNATURE OF PATIENT (or person authorized to sign on patient's behalf)   DATE

Authorization for the Release of Financial Records

I,_____, hereby authorize _____

_____Insurance Company, or its agents _____

to obtain copies of any and all financial or other pertinent records, wherever

situated, pertaining to me. Such records may include, by way of example and not

of limitation, any and all charge-account records, credit history reports, checking-

account records, savings-account records, promissory notes, employment

records, insurance records, rental or lease records, business records involving

businesses owned or operated by me, accounting records, telephone records,

utility records and financial statements concerning me or any business operated

or owned by me.

A copy of this release shall have the same force and effect as the original.

Date:_____ 199____

Signature:_____

Witness:_____

Insurance Company

Address

City, State, Zip

Logo

To Whom It May Concern:

I, _____, do hereby authorize

_____ Insurance Company Representative

to obtain all the wage information from the time period

_____.

I also authorize _____

to release this information.

Signature:_____

Date:_____

Reasons Why a Worker's Compensation Claim May Not be Compensable

It is critical that the rules of the worker's compensation board or authority in the investigator's area of operation be referred to when interpreting any of these possible denials of compensability.

1. *Injury did not happen on the job.* Beware of the 8 a.m. Monday morning injury. It may have happened on the weekend. A check of local hospital admissions, neighbors or recreation leagues may turn up leads that a claimant was injured in a place other than work.

2. *Going and coming.* Normally, when an employee is going to or from work, an injury incurred is not covered by worker's compensation. Exceptions may include situations where an employer pays an allowance or provides a company vehicle specifically for commuting.

3. *Deviation from normal duties.* If a salesperson is disabled from lifting a hundred-pound box of brochures, did he or she really have to do it as part of his or her job? Was the action that caused the injury considered to be a regular, expected job-duty of the employee?

4. *Personal errand rule.* If an employee leaves work for nonwork-related reasons, an injury may not be compensable.

5. *An injury that is self-inflicted.* Although it is tough to disprove the intentions of the employee, the investigator should be aware that this occurs and that if it can be proven that the injury was intentional, the claim may possibly be denied.

An accident at work caused by horseplay may not be compensable.

6. *Goofing around.* If an employee is hurt while engaged in horseplay unrelated to job activities, the claim may not be compensable.

7. *Criminal claimant behavior.* A claimant injured while knowingly involved in illicit activities while at the workplace might not be covered under the worker's compensation policy of the insured.

8. *Use of drugs or alcohol.* Be careful here, for intoxication may have to be the overwhelming issue, with no other factors contributing to the accident.

9. *Statutes of limitations for filing a claim have expired.* Check federal and state statutes to determine policies on expiration dates within the insured's area of operation.

10. *Suicide or mysterious death.* Check local statues to determine if, for instance, someone found dead from drug or alcohol use on the job qualifies for compensation benefits.

There are other reasons a claim may be denied or benefits reduced. This is usually the area where the expertise of the adjustor comes into play. The previous ten points are the most obvious for an SIU checklist.

Medical Provider Fraud

Provider fraud is steadily being recognized as a serious and extremely expensive abuse costing insurance companies and the general public millions of dollars per year. SIU investigators identifying providers who abuse the worker's compensation and personal injury system can not only save their company from excessive payouts, but do a favor for the average citizen who ultimately pays for fraudulent activity through higher premiums.

A multitude of fraudulent behavior can be classed under the provider fraud heading. Included are medical or provider "mills" that process hundreds, even thousands of worker's compensation and liability claims. Some law offices and clinics even hire "cappers" who recruit potential claimants from unemployment lines in order to file stress or injury claims. Individual providers or their clinics can bill for unnecessary or unperformed treatments, charge multiple agencies for services performed and bill excessively through upcoding. Upcoding refers to the provider or clinic applying a procedure code for a higher level of medical service than that which was performed.

PROVIDER FRAUD/BILLING ABUSE

The following list is intended to give both SIU staffers and claims personnel a general indication of the types of potentially fraudulent behavior that can be associated with medical provider fraud. As this type of fraud can be both complicated and steeped in unfamiliar terminology, the investigator should consult as many resources as possible when familiarizing with and even investigating provider activity. These resources could include consultation with doctors respected in their fields, medical peer review board members, other investigators with experience in dealing with potential provider fraud and even consumer organizations who monitor cost issues associated with the medical profession. Other sources may include state fraud bureaus and

Aggressive, questionable advertising has propelled the growth of "Injury Mills."

organizations such as the National Insurance Crime Bureau (NICB) which may have data or information concerning potentially fraudulent medical provider activity.

Medical provider fraud and billing abuses can include:

- Provider bills for medical services not actually performed.

- Provider submits multiple bills for the same service to more than one party responsible for bill payment (insurance company, Medicare, etc.). The provider can also submit multiple bills to the same insurance company or party responsible for payment using creative billing methods. Also known as *double billing*.

- Physician assigns a procedure code for a higher level of treatment than was performed, creating a higher cost for that service. Also known as *upcoding*.

- Misrepresentation of the diagnosis code. In order to insure that a procedure or treatment will be covered by insurance, the physician provides an inappropriate diagnosis to insure coverage.

- Billing for services not covered by insurance policy. The provider creatively bills for services which may not be covered (weight loss treatments, smoke cessation, or other non-conventional or controversial treatments).

- Healthcare provider bills insurance company for medical treatments as if they were performed by that provider, when in actuality the services were performed by other personnel. If this type of activity is revealed, licensing of personnel performing these services should also be scrutinized.

- Billing for services not considered medically necessary.

- Provider bills a medical procedure by its individual components rather than as a whole, generating additional revenue because the parts (billed individually) have a higher rate of reimbursement than when billed as one major procedure. Also known as *unbundling*.

- Healthcare provider refers patients to several other providers who perform and bill for similar services. Sometimes referred to as *pingponging* patients.

- Provider does not attempt to collect co-payment from patient or waives it altogether. With no co-pay, the patient assumes little or no financial responsibility for treatment, thus encouraging the patient to continue services.

- Healthcare provider or hospital representative provides an insurance company with inaccurate information in order to receive pre-authorization or pre-certification for admission to that hospital (Pre-authorization and pre-certification are often necessary to ensure insurance coverage).

Red Flags, Indicators of Potential Insurance Fraud

The checklists that follow, compiled by the NICB, can be used when training claims personnel as well as special investigators in the detection of potentially fraudulent insurance claims. It should be noted that the majority of insurance claims are legitimate. All individuals working in the claims-handling field nonetheless should be well versed in identifying claims that may be suspicious or in need of more detailed investigation.

The indicators, commonly referred to as "red flags," are suggestions that a closer look be taken into the merits of a specific claim. Special investigators may request that a claims adjustor refer a file to the SIU if one or even several of the red flags crop up on any single claim. The potential for further investigation then can be determined, as well as a course of action for the investigator assigned to look into the matter. The NICB requests that all suspicious claims be reported to its organization regardless of the outcome of the investigation. The NICB can be contacted for further information at (708) 430-2430.

The NICB is a critical component of the concerted industry-wide fight against claim fraud. It has cooperated with law-enforcement agencies to solve crimes both directly and indirectly related to insurance fraud.

Indicators of Potential Worker's Compensation Fraud

Worker's compensation fraud is fast becoming one of the most well-known areas with the potential for abuse in the insurance industry. The list that follows concentrates on claimant fraud within the worker's compensation system. Claims adjustors recognizing one or more red flags on a worker's compensation claim should consult with their SIU to determine the best methods of investigation.

THE CLAIMANT, PRIOR CLAIM HISTORY AND CURRENT WORK STATUS

The following indicators should be considered if the:

- Injured worker is disgruntled, soon-to-retire, or facing imminent firing or layoff.

- Injured worker is involved in seasonal work that is about to end.

- Injured worker took unexplained or excessive time off prior to claimed injury.

- Injured worker takes more time off than the claimed injury seems to warrant.

- Injured worker is nomadic and has a history of short-term employment.

- Injured worker is new on the job.

- Injured worker is experiencing financial difficulties.

- Injured worker recently purchased private disability policies.

- Injured worker changes physician when a release for work has been issued.

- Injured worker has a history of reporting subjective injuries.

- Review of a rehab report describes the claimant as being muscular, well tanned, with callused hands and grease under the fingernails.

CIRCUMSTANCES OF THE ACCIDENT

- Accident occurs late Friday afternoon or shortly after the employee reports to work on Monday.

- Accident is unwitnessed.

- Claimant has leg/arm injuries at odd time, i.e. at lunch hour.

- Fellow workers hear rumors circulating that accident was not legitimate.

- Accident occurs in an area where injured employee would not normally be.

- Accident is not the type that the employee should be involved in, i.e. an office worker who is lifting heavy objects on a loading dock.

- Accident occurs just prior to a strike, or near end of probationary period.

- Employer's first report of claim contradicts with description of accident set forth in medical history.

- Details of accident are vague.

- Incident is not promptly reported by employee to supervisor.

- Surveillance or "tip" reveals the totally disabled worker is currently employed elsewhere.

- After injury, injured worker is never home or spouse/relative answering phone states the injured worked "just stepped out."

- Return calls to residence have strange or unexpected background noises.

MEDICAL TREATMENT

- Diagnosis is inconsistent with treatment.

- Physician is known for handling suspect claims.

- Treatment for extensive injuries is protracted though the accident was minor.

- "Boilerplate" medical reports are identical to other reports from the same doctor.

- Workers' compensation insurer and health carrier are billed simultaneously; payments are accepted from both.

- Injured worker protests about returning to work and never seems to improve.

- Summary medical bills submitted without dates or descriptions of office visits.

- Medical bills submitted are photocopies of originals.

- Extensive or unnecessary treatments for minor, subjective injuries.

- Treatment directed to separate facility in which the referring physician has a financial interest (especially if this is not disclosed in advance).

- Referral for treatment/testing to facility close to referring facility.

- Injuries are all subjective, i.e. pain, headaches, nausea, inability to sleep.

- Injured worker cancels or fails to keep appointment, or refuses a diagnostic procedure to confirm an injury.

- Treatment dates appear on holidays or other days that facilities would not normally be open.

- Injured worker is immediately referred for a wide variety of psychiatric tests, when the original claim involved trauma only. These usually present with vague complaints of "stress."

THE CLAIMANT'S ATTORNEY

- Attorney is known for handling suspicious claims.

- Attorney lien or representation letter dated the day of the reported incident.

- Same doctor/lawyer pair previously observed to handle this kind of injury.

- Claimant complains to carrier's CEO at home office to press for payment.

- Claimant initially wants to settle with insurer, but later retains an attorney with increased subjective complaints.

- Pattern of occupational type claims for "dying" industries, i.e. black lung, asbestos; wholesale claim handling by law firms and multiple class action suits.

- Attorney threatens further legal action unless a quick settlement is made.

- High incidence of applications from a specific firm.

- Attorney inquires about a settlement or buyout early in the life of the claim.

Indicators of Potential Casualty Fraud

Casualty fraud in the insurance arena can take many forms. Familiarity with the following "red flags" can lead to early detection and intervention of potentially fraudulent behavior. General indications of insurance fraud, included in the following list, can be applied to many areas within the industry. Also included are sections for the detection of fraud in automobile accident schemes, claim inflation, lost earnings fraud, slip and falls and product liability. Please refer any suspicious claims to the NICB regardless of the outcome of the investigation.

GENERAL INDICATORS OF INSURANCE FRAUD

- Claimant or insured is excessively eager to accept blame for an accident, or is overly pushy or demanding of a quick, reduced settlement.

- Claimant or insured is unusually familiar with insurance terms and procedure, medical, or vehicle repair terminology.

- One or more claimants or insured list a post office box or hotel as address.

- All transactions were conducted in person; claimant avoids using the telephone or the mail.

- The kind of accident or type of vehicles involved are not typical of those seen on a regular basis.

- Claimant threatens to go to an attorney or physician if the claim is not quickly settled.

- Claimant is a transient or out-of-towner on vacation.

INDICATORS OF AUTOMOBILE ACCIDENT SCHEMES

- Either no police report or an over-the-counter report for an accident resulting in multiple injuries and/or extensive physical damage.

- Accident occurred shortly after one or more of the vehicles were purchased or registered, or after the addition of comprehensive and collision coverage to the policy.

- Insured has a history of accidents within a short period of time on one policy. Index returns indicate an active claim history.

- Insured has no record of prior insurance coverage although damaged vehicle was purchased much earlier than inception of policy and date of loss.

- Expensive, late model automobile was recently purchased with cash (no lienholder.)

- Attorney's lien or representation letter is dated the day of the accident or soon after.

AUTOMOBILE PHYSICAL DAMAGE FRAUD INDICATORS

- Serious accident with expensive physical damage claim but only minor, subjectively diagnosed injuries, with little or no medical treatment.

- Despite expensive damage claims, the claimant vehicle remains drivable. Often, there are no towing charges for removing vehicle from the scene of the accident.

- Claimant vehicle is not to be repaired locally, but driven or shipped out of state for repair.

- All vehicles in a reported accident are taken to the same body shop.

- Claimant vehicles are not readily available for independent appraisal.

- Reported accident occurred on private property near residence of those involved.

MEDICAL FRAUD/CLAIM INFLATION INDICATORS

- Three or more occupants in the claimant or "struck vehicle"; all of them report similar injuries.

- All injuries are subjectively diagnosed, such as headaches, muscle spasms, traumas, and others.

- Medical claims are extensive, but collision is minor with little physical damage to the vehicles.

- All of the claimants submit medical bills from the same doctor or medical facility.

- Medical bills submitted are photocopies of the originals.

- Summary of medical bills are submitted without dates and descriptions of office visits and treatments, or treatment extends for a lengthy period without any interim bills.

- Vehicle driven by claimant is an old "clunker" with minimal coverage.

- Insured, even though legally liable for accident, is adamant that claimants were responsible for accident, indicating that the insured may have been "targeted" by the claimants.

- Claimants retain legal representation immediately after the accident is reported.

- Minor accident produces major medical costs, lost wages and unusually expensive demands for pain and suffering.

- Past experience demonstrates that the physician's bill and report, regardless of the varying accident circumstances, is always the same.

- Treatment prescribed for the various injuries resulting from differing accidents is always the same in terms of duration and type of therapy.

- Medical bills indicate routine treatment being provided on Sundays and holidays.

INDICATORS OF LOST EARNINGS FRAUD

- Employment information is for an unknown business, often with a post office box for address, or a street address in a residential area.

- Business telephone number is connected to an answering machine or answering service.

- Lost earnings statement is handwritten or typed on blank paper, not business letterhead.

- Claimant started employment shortly before accident occurred, or is self-employed.

- One or more elements of claim is questionable: e.g. length of absence, rate of pay, income incompatible with claimant's residence.

- Efforts to verify lost wage statement with employer raise doubts about employer's legitimacy or about the actual employment of the claimant.

SLIP AND FALL, FOOD/PRODUCTS LIABILITY

- Presence of an overly enthusiastic witness at the scene of the incident.

- No supporting evidence of foreign or contaminated substance; claimant threw food out and has only the can, box or wrapper.

Indicators of Potential Property Fraud

Many variables could indicate the need for further investigation into a property file because of possibly fraudulent behavior. Following are "red flags" for arson and other fire-related claims, burglary and theft claims and other general indications that closer scrutiny may be necessary. As always, the NICB requests that all suspicious claims be reported to its organization regardless of the outcome of the investigation.

GENERAL INDICATORS OF PROPERTY FRAUD

- Insured is overly pushy for a quick settlement.

- Insured is unusually knowledgeable regarding insurance terminology and the claims settlement process.

- Insured handles all business in person, thus avoiding the use of the mail.

- Insured is willing to accept an inordinately small settlement rather than document all claims losses.

- Insured contacts agent to verify coverage or extend coverage just prior to loss date.

- Insured is recently separated or divorced.

- Suspiciously coincidental absence of insured or family at the time of the incident.

- Losses occur just after coverage takes effect, just before it ceases or just after it has been increased.

- Losses are incompatible with insured's residence, occupation and/or income.

- Losses include a large amount of cash.

- Commercial losses that primarily involve seasonal inventory or equipment, and that occur at the end of the selling season, e.g. a ski inventory loss in the spring or a farm machinery loss in the fall.

ARSON-FOR-PROFIT, FIRE-RELATED FRAUD INDICATORS

Note: While arson-for-profit is unquestionably the most costly economic assault on the property insurance industry, claims handlers also should be aware of fraud occurring when an insured takes criminal advantage of an accidental fire.

- Building and/or contents were up for sale at the time of the loss.

- Suspiciously coincidental absence of family pet at time of fire.

- Insured had a loss at the same site within the preceding year. The initial loss, though small, may have been a failed attempt to liquidate contents.

- Building and/or business was recently purchased.

- Commercial losses include old and non-saleable inventory or illegal chemicals/materials. Insured or insured's business is experiencing financial difficulties, e.g. bankruptcy, foreclosure.

- Fire site is claimed by multiple mortgagees or chattel mortgagees.

INDICATORS AT THE FIRE SCENE

- Building is in deteriorating condition and/or located in a deteriorating neighborhood.

- Fire scene investigation suggests that property/contents were heavily over-insured.

- Fire scene investigation reveals absence of remains of non-combustible items of scheduled property or items covered by floaters, e.g. coin or gun collections or jewelry.

- Fire scene investigation reveals absence of remains of expensive items used to justify an increase over normal 50% contents coverage, e.g. antiques, piano, or expensive stereo/video equipment.

- Fire scene investigation reveals absence of items of sentimental value: e.g. family Bible, family photos, trophies.

- Fire scene investigation reveals absence of remains of items normally found in a home or business. The following is a sample listing of such items, most of which will be identifiable at fire scenes except in total burns. Kitchen: major appliances, minor appliances, normal food supply in refrigerator and cabinets. Living Room: television/stereo equipment, record/tape collections, organ or piano, furniture (springs will remain). Bedroom: guns, jewelry, clothing and toys. Basement/Garage: tools, lawn mower, bicycles, sporting equipment, e.g. golf clubs (especially note if putter is missing from otherwise complete set). Business/Office: office equipment and furniture, normal inventory, business records (which are normally housed in metal filing cabinets and should survive most fires).

INDICATORS ASSOCIATED WITH THE LOSS INCIDENT

- Fire occurs at night, especially after 11:00 p.m.

- Commercial fire occurs on holiday, weekend or when business is closed.

- Fire department reports fire cause is incendiary, suspicious or unknown.

- Fire alarm and/or sprinkler system failed to work at the time of the loss.

INDICATORS OF BURGLARY/THEFT FRAUD

- Losses include total contents of business/home including items of little or no value.

- Losses are questionable, e.g. home stereo stolen out of car, fur coat stolen on trip to Hawaii.

- Losses include numerous family heirlooms.

- Losses include numerous appraised items and/or items of scheduled property.

- Extensive commercial losses occur at site where few or no security measures are in effect.

- No police report or over-the-counter report in situations where police would normally investigate.

INDICATORS ASSOCIATED WITH
THE CLAIMS PROCESS

- Insured over-documents losses with a receipt for every loss and/or older items of property.

- Insured's loss inventory differs significantly from policy department's crime report.

- Insured cannot provide receipts, cancelled checks or other proof of ownership for recently purchased items.

- Insured provides numerous receipts for inexpensive items, but no receipts for items of significant value.

- Insured provides receipt(s) with incorrect or no sales tax figures.

- Insured provides receipt(s) with no store logo (blank receipt).

- Loss inventory indicates unusually high number of recent purchases.

- Insured cannot recall place and/or date of purchase of newer items of significant value.

- Insured indicates distress over prospect of an examination under oath.

- Insured cannot provide bank or credit card records for recent purchases of significant value.

- Insured provides receipts/invoices from same supplier that are numbered in sequence.

- Insured provides two different receipts with same handwriting or typeface.

- Insured provides single receipt with different handwriting or typefaces.

- Insured provides credit card receipts with incorrect or no approval code.

Indicators of Potential Vehicle Theft Fraud

The "Red flags" that follow include possible fraudulent activity on the part of the insured, reporting the theft of the vehicle, vehicle coverage and the actual vehicle itself. As with other types of fraudulent behavior within the insurance industry, the NICB requests that all vehicle thefts and sales of total loss salvage sold by insurance companies or left in claimant possession at settlement time be reported to its organization. If the vehicle is an expensive sports car, truck-tractor or any other valuable or luxury model, please include the current and four preceding model years as well as older model years for total loss salvage.

INDICATORS OF FRAUD CONCERNING THE INSURED

- Insured has lived at current address less than six months.

- Insured has been with current employer less than six months.

- Insured's address is a post office box or mail drop.

- Insured does not have a telephone.

- Insured's listed number is a mobile/cellular phone.

- Insured is difficult to contact.

- Insured frequently changes address and/or phone number.

- Insured's place of contact is a hotel, tavern, or other place which is neither his/her place of employment nor place of residence.

- Insured conducts all business in person, does not use mails.

- Insured is unemployed.

- Insured claims to be self-employed but is vague about the business and actual responsibilities.
- Insured has recent or current marital and/or financial problems.
- Insured has a temporary, recently issued, or out-of-state driver's license.
- Insured's driver's license has recently been suspended.
- Insured recently called to confirm and/or increase coverage.
- Insured has an accumulation of parking tickets on vehicle.
- Insured is unusually aggressive and pressures for quick settlement.
- Insured offers inducement for quick settlement.
- Insured is very knowledgeable of claims process and insurance terminology.
- Insured's income is not compatible with value of insured vehicle.
- Insured claims expensive contents in vehicle at time of theft.
- Insured is employed with another insurance company.
- Insured wants a friend or relative to pick up settlement check.
- Insured is behind in loan payments on vehicle and/or financial obligations.
- Insured avoids meetings with investigators and/or claims adjustors.
- Insured cancels scheduled appointments with claims adjustors for statements and/or examination under oath.
- Insured has previous history of vehicle theft claims.

INDICATORS OF FRAUD RELATING TO THE VEHICLE

- Vehicle was purchased for cash with no bill of sale or proof of ownership.
- Vehicle is a new or late model with no lien holder.
- Vehicle was recently purchased.
- Vehicle was not seen for an extended period of time prior to the reported theft.

- Vehicle was purchased out of state.
- Vehicle has a history of mechanical problems.
- Vehicle is a "gas guzzler."
- Vehicle is customized, classic, and/or antique.
- Vehicle displayed "for sale" signs prior to theft.
- Vehicle was recovered clinically/carefully stripped.
- Vehicle is parked on street although garage is available.
- Vehicle was recovered stripped, but insured wants to retain salvage, and repair appears to be impractical.
- Vehicle is recovered by the insured or a friend.
- Vehicle purchase price was exceptionally high or low.
- Vehicle was recovered with old or recent damage and coverage was high deductible or no collision coverage.
- Vehicle coverage is only on a binder.
- Vehicle has an incorrect VIN (e.g. not originally manufactured, inconsistent with model).
- Vehicle was a General Motors conversion diesel engine model.
- Vehicle VIN is different than VIN appearing on the title.
- Vehicle VIN provided to police is incorrect.
- Federal vehicle safety certification label is altered or missing.
- Federal vehicle safety certification label displays different VIN than is displayed on vehicle.
- Vehicle has theft and/or salvage history.
- Vehicle is recovered with no ignition or steering lock damage.
- Vehicle is recovered with seized engine or blown transmission.
- Vehicle was previously involved in a major collision.
- Vehicle is late model with extremely high mileage (exceptions: taxi, police, utility vehicles).
- Vehicle is older model with exceptionally low mileage (i.e. odometer rollover/rollback).

- Vehicle is older or inexpensive model and insured indicates it was equipped with expensive accessories which cannot be substantiated with receipts.

- Vehicle is recovered stripped, burned, or has severe collision damage within a short duration of time after loss allegedly occurred.

- Leased vehicle with excessive mileage for which the insured would have been liable under the mileage limitation agreement.

INDICATORS OF
FRAUD RELATED TO AUTO COVERAGE

- Loss occurs within one month of issue or expiration of the policy.

- Loss occurs after cancellation notice was sent to insured.

- Insurance premium was paid in cash.

- Coverage obtained via walk-in business to agent.

- Coverage obtained from an agent not located in close proximity to insured's residence or work place.

- Coverage is for minimum liability with full comprehensive coverage on late model and/or expensive vehicle.

- Coverage was recently increased.

FRAUD INDICATORS
RELATED TO REPORTING

- Police report has not been made by insured or has been delayed.

- No report or claim is made to insurance carrier within one week after theft.

- Neighbors, friends, and family are not aware of loss.

- License plate does not match vehicle and/or is not registered to insured.

- Title is junk, salvage, out-of-state, photocopied, or duplicated.

- Title history shown non-existent addresses.

- Repair bills are consecutively numbered or dates show work accomplished on weekends or holidays.

- An individual, rather than a bank or financial institution, is named as the lien holder.

GENERAL INDICATORS OF
VEHICLE THEFT FRAUD

- Vehicle is towed to isolated yard at owner's request.

- Salvage yard or repair garage takes unusual interest in claim.

- Information concerning prior owner is unavailable.

- Prior owner cannot be located.

- Vehicle is recovered totally burned after theft.

- Fire damage is inconsistent with loss description.

- VINs were removed prior to fire.

Indicators of Potential Application Fraud

When applying for insurance coverage, the majority of individuals do so honestly. Some applicants, however, do so with the intent to deceive. To avoid potentially problematic claims in the future, agents and adjustors should be aware of the "red flags" that follow, as well as SIU staffers who may later be called on for their investigative services.

GENERAL INDICATORS OF APPLICATION FRAUD

- Unsolicited, new walk-in business not referred by any existing policyholder.

- Applicant walks into agent's office at noon or at the end of the day when the agent and staff may be rushed.

- Applicant neither works nor resides near the agency.

- Applicant's given address is inconsistent with employment/income.

- Applicant gives post office box as an address.

- Applicant has lived at current address less than six months.

- Applicant has no telephone number or provides a mobile/cellular phone number.

- Applicant cannot provide driver's license or other identification or has temporary, recently issued, or out-of-state driver's license.

- Applicant wants to pay the premium in cash.

- Applicant pays minimum required amount of premium.

- Applicant suggests price is no object when applying for coverage.

- Applicant's income is not compatible with the value of the vehicle to be insured.

- Applicant is never available to meet in person and supplies all information by telephone.

- Applicant is unemployed or self-employed in a transient occupation (e.g. roofing, asphalt).

- Applicant questions agent closely on claim handling procedures.

- Applicant is unusually familiar with insurance terms or procedures.

- Application is not signed in the agent's view (e.g. mailed in).

- Applicant is reluctant to use mail.

- Applicant works through a third party.

- Applicant returns the completed application unsigned.

- Applicant has had driver's license for significant period, but no prior vehicle ownership and/or insurance.

INDICATORS ASSOCIATED WITH COVERAGE

- Name of the previous insurance carrier or proof of prior coverage cannot be provided.

- No prior insurance coverage is reported although applicant's age would suggest prior ownership of a vehicle and/or property.

- Significant break-in coverage is reported under prior coverage.

- Question about recent prior claims are left unanswered.

- Full coverage is requested for older vehicle.

- No existing damage is reported for older vehicle.

- Exceptionally high liability limits are requested for older vehicle inconsistent with applicant's employment, income or lifestyle.

INDICATORS ASSOCIATED WITH APPLICANT'S VEHICLE/BUSINESS

- Vehicle is not available for inspection.

- Photos are submitted in lieu of inspection.

- Vehicle does not appear to be appropriate for claimed address or income (e.g. a luxury vehicle in a low income neighborhood).

- Vehicle has an unusual amount of aftermarket equipment (e.g. wheels, high priced stereo, CB radio, car phone).

- Vehicle inspection by agent uncovers discrepancy between VIN listed on title/bill of sale, VIN plate on the dashboard, and/or manufacturer's sticker on door.

- No lien holder is reported for new and/or high value vehicle.

- Vehicle title or an authenticated bill of sale cannot be produced.

- Applicant is seeking new business coverage and has never been in any, or this type of, business in the past.

- Sound financial backing for the business to be insured is not apparent.

- Loss payee is not a legitimate lending institution (e.g. banks or finance company).

Glossary

This chapter is by no means an all-encompassing insurance term lexicon, but it is dedicated to those working in the arena of fraud investigations.

ALJ Administrative law judge. A hearing officer or examiner presiding over such matters as worker's compensation proceedings.

AOE/COE Arising Out of Employment, in the Course Of Employment; usually refers to an incident taking place as a result of being on the job and the ensuing investigation to determine the potential compensability of a claim.

ABUSE OF PROCESS Abusing the legal system, often by excessive litigation, unnecessary motions and procedures or sometimes by actual harassment.

ACTION IN DECEIT A court or legal action in which damages may be collected as a remedy for fraudulent acts.

ADDITUR A court-mandated increase of an "inadequate" jury award. This is sometimes done to deny a plaintiff's motion for another trial or appeal.

ADJUSTOR Also known as claims handler, claim representative. The insurance company employee responsible for handling the claim file once the claim has been reported by the insured. Adjustors often are the first line of defense against claim fraud, recognizing red flags and ultimately working with SIU personnel and private vendors to determine the validity of a claim.

ALIAS Assumed name.

ALLEGATION A statement or assertion not having yet been substantiated.

ALLOCATED CLAIM EXPENSE Costs of administering a claims file including legal and investigative expenses. Does not include indemnity dollar payouts.

The Discovery Process often yields more than meets the eye.

APPLICANT In worker's compensation, one who applies for benefits.

ARBITRATION The process of negotiating a settlement amount for a particular action. Arbitration can be binding or non-binding.

BI Bodily injury.

CAPPER, CHASER Individuals working for a mill operator who recruit potential claimants, referring them to various individuals associated with the mill operation.

CLAIMANT A person who files or turns in a claim. Often referred to as the "subject" during an investigation and as the "plaintiff" once suit has been filed.

COMPROMISE AND RELEASE Also known as a C-and-R document, the Compromise and Release is a paper that normally absolves the past employer of any future liability after settling the case with a lump-sum payout.

CONTINUANCE A judge or arbitrator's delaying action on a particular case or hearing. A later date usually is rescheduled for further review of the matter in question.

CONTRIBUTORY Short for contributory negligence or actions of the claimant that might have contributed to the accident happening in the first place. In some states, a jury verdict is reduced by the percentage of negligence contributed by the claimant.

COVERT Under cover; a method of investigation used to gather information in a low-key manner, not usually arousing the suspicions of the subject.

DAMAGES Worker's compensation or liability payments awarded to a claimant for actual losses (as opposed to punitive, potential or possible damages).

DEDUCTIBLE The amount that an insured is liable to pay before the policy provides coverage.

DISCOVERY The process of discovering the facts surrounding the plaintiff's case. The discovery process includes depositions, statements, document review and affidavits.

EUO Examination under oath.

EARNINGS The average income of an injured party in a worker's compensation or general liability claim. This figure is significant in determining the potential reimbursement rates for the claimant.

EXPERIENCE MOD The insured's history of claim loss as expressed in a ratio. Used to determine premiums and safety levels of a company.

EXPOSURE The level to which the company is exposed to the loss. For instance, in worker's compensation, the exposure may be medical payments plus lost time plus loss of future earnings. The term also may apply to policy limits.

FRAUD An intentional misrepresentation of facts fabricated with the intent of deceiving or cheating another.

GL General Liability claim.

GROSS NEGLIGENCE Actions committed without regard to the body or property of another. May be an important factor in attributing responsibility in a claim.

HEARSAY Rumor or secondhand information. Often inadmissible as evidence unless corroborated by other witnesses.

ID In surveillance, ID means identification, as in "do the tapes have good ID?" Proper claimant identification is extremely important prior to taking any action on a file based on surveillance videotapes and other evidence.

IME Independent medical exam. Usually an independent exam conducted by a physician chosen by the claims department. Also known as an AME or agreed medical examination.

LUMP SUM, OR "LUMP IT OUT" A settlement given all at once, often with the purpose of cutting off a long-term series of indemnity dollar payments. To "lump the case out" is to close the file by way of this payment.

LTD: Long-term disability.

MILL An establishment, usually medical or automotive body shop, that specializes in running through many human or automobile bodies with the same, repetitious routine. The volume of business of these operations may be an indication that suspect claims are being routinely processed.

Hearsay Evidence is often inadmissable.

Mills that process claimants like commodities sometimes have encouraged excessive costs on claim files.

PI Personal injury.

PPD Permanent partial disability. A disability with long-term lingering effects that are not fully or totally disabling (less than 100 percent).

PTD Permanent and total disability.

PRETEXT Investigative technique utilizing a disguised identity to obtain information that might not be forthcoming if a more forthright approach were taken.

RED FLAGS A series of indicators that may suggest the need for a more detailed investigation of a claim. Several "hits" may indicate potentially fraudulent behavior or action in regards to a particular claim or claims.

REINSURANCE Insurance purchased by an insurer to spread the risk of a particular policy among more than one insurer.

RELEASE Authorization form allowing access to what may otherwise be privileged information.

RESPONDEAT SUPERIOR The doctrine that holds that one who hires another may be at least partially responsible for the actions of that firm or person. May be an issue if a vendor conducts an investigation in an unprofessional or overzealous manner. Contingent liability is another way to express the exposure.

SIU Special Investigation Unit. The division of an insurance company responsible for the investigation of potentially fraudulent claims. Other duties include heightening the awareness of fraud issues through training claims staff and even the general public.

STAGED ACCIDENTS Purposeful collisions created with the intent of defrauding the insurance company.

STRUCTURED SETTLEMENT A method of claim settlement using a variety of financial instruments (such as annuities) to provide the claimant support over a long-term period into the future.

SUB ROSA Investigative method using a low-key approach to avoid subject awareness. Pretext often is an intrinsic part of this technique.

TPD Temporary partial disability. Disability benefits awarded to any employee who can work in a light-duty situation, part-time or in any other modified-duty situation.

TTD Temporary total disability. Benefits paid to any employee who is physically unable to perform any type of gainful employment. The employee would be considered medically excused from employment because of his or her injury.

TORT An act that might be remedied through legal recourse. From an investigator's point of view, keep in mind that insurance usually covers unintentional torts, not purposeful ones.

TOTAL LOSS What you would experience if you had a hot-air balloon that you forgot to deflate before the hurricane came through town.

VIN Vehicle identification number.

VENDOR Supplier of services to the insurer. Vendors most frequently dealt with by SIU personnel include private investigation companies, cause and origin investigators and accident reconstructionists.

VOC REHAB Vocational rehabilitation. A service with which an injured employee can be trained to perform another task or job duty that is not related to the original job description. This service is performed with the goal of returning the injured employee to the workplace in another capacity.

WAGE LOSS Benefits paid to an injured employee who has returned to his or her place of employment to perform light or modified-duty work or also in a part-time capacity.

WORKER'S COMPENSATION The process or system developed to compensate an employee for injuries occurring during the course of the employee's employment or arising out of that employment.

Insurance Fraud Hotline Directory

This list has been compiled and provided by the National Council on Compensation Insurance, Inc. (NCCI). To report any type of suspected worker's compensation premium/employer fraud, in any NCCI jurisdiction, contact:

> NCCI
> Two Tamarac Square
> 7535 East Hampden Avenue, Suite 613
> Denver, CO 80231
> (303) 368-7730 or (303) 695-8891

ALABAMA

To report suspected worker's compensation claims fraud (including bogus claims, improper billing, etc.), contact:

> The Worker's Compensation Division
> Department of Industrial Relations
> Industrial Relations Building
> Montgomery, AL 36130
> (205) 242-2868

To report suspected agent or insurance company fraud, contact:

> The State of Alabama
> Department of Insurance Consumer Services
> Administrative Building, Room 453
> 135 South Union Street
> Montgomery, AL 36130-3401
> (205) 269-3550

Insurance fraud hotlines are direct lines
set up to prevent insurance abuse.

ALASKA

To report any suspected worker's compensation fraud, contact:

State of Alaska
Division of Insurance
800 East Diamond Boulevard, Suite 560
Anchorage, AK 99515
(907) 349-1230
Fax: (907) 349-1280

ARIZONA

To report suspected claims fraud, contact:.

Arizona Industrial Commission
800 West Washington Street
Phoenix, AZ 85007
(602) 542-4411

To report suspected agent or insurance company fraud, contact:

Arizona State Department of Insurance
Attn.: Consumer Affairs
3030 North Third Street, Suite 1100
Phoenix, AZ 85012
(602) 255-4783

ARKANSAS

To report suspected claims or medical provider fraud in Arkansas, all allegations must be specific and in writing and sent to the address below for referral to the appropriate insurance company.

Arkansas Worker's Compensation Commission
Justice Building, 2nd Floor
625 Marshall Street
Little Rock, AR 72201-1073

To report suspected worker's compensation fraud by agents, employers, and insurance companies, contact:

Arkansas Department of Insurance
400 University Tower Building
Little Rock, AR 72204
(501) 686-2999

CALIFORNIA

To report all types of suspected worker's compensation fraud, contact the appropriate California Fraud Bureau office in your region:

Fraud Division
State of California
Department of Insurance
7100 Bowling Drive, Suite 400
Sacramento, CA 95823
(916) 323-1363

Fraud Division
State of California
Department of Insurance
107 South Broadway, Suite 9111
Los Angeles, CA 90012
(213) 897-8861

Fraud Division
State of California
Department of Insurance
1340 Arnold Drive, Suite 220
Martinez, CA 94553
(510) 313-8800

To report suspected medical provider worker's compensation fraud, contact:

Department of Consumer Affairs
Medical Board of California
1426 Howe Avenue
Sacramento, CA 95825-3236
Toll-free complaint hotline (inside California): 1-800-633-2322

COLORADO

To report suspected worker's compensation fraud, contact:

Compliance Investigations
Colorado Compensation Insurance Authority
P.O. Box 241303
Denver, CO 80024-9303
(303) 782-4053
Toll-free hotline: 1-800-873-1888

To report suspected worker's compensation claims fraud, contact:

Colorado Department of Labor & Employment
Investigations and Criminal Enforcement
600 Grant Street, Suite 900
Denver, CO 80203-3528
(303) 837-3806

To report all types of insurance fraud, including worker's compensation, contact:

The Colorado Insurance Fraud Coalition (not a state agency)
1-800-888-8043 (inside Colorado)

CONNECTICUT

To report all types of suspected worker's compensation fraud, contact:

Worker's Compensation Fraud Unit
Office of the Chief Attorney
340 Quinnipiac Street
Wallingford, CT 06492
(203) 265-2373

DELAWARE

To report suspected fraudulent claims to the appropriate insurance company, call:

The Delaware Industrial Accident Board
State Office Building, 6th Floor
820 North French Street
Wilmington, DE 19801
(302) 577-2884

The Delaware Industrial Accident Board can provide you with the name of the insurance carrier in each specific case so that you can report the suspected fraud directly to the insurance company for investigation.

DISTRICT OF COLUMBIA

To report suspected worker's compensation claims fraud (including bogus claims, improper billing, etc.), contact:

The Department of Employment Services
Office of Worker's Compensation
P.O. Box 56098
Washington, D.C. 20011
(202) 576-6265

To report suspected fraud by an agent or insurance company, contact:

Government of the District of Columbia
Department of Consumer & Regulatory Affairs
Insurance Administration
Fraud Bureau
P.O. Box 37200
Washington, D.C. 20013-7200
(202) 727-8017

FLORIDA

To report any suspected worker's compensation fraud in Florida, contact the nearest Florida Bureau of Worker's Compensation Fraud office:

Tallahassee (headquarters)
200 East Gaines Street
(mailing address)
649 Fletcher Building
(physical address)
Tallahassee, FL 32399-0300
(904) 922-3116
Suncom: 292-3116
Fax: (904) 488-2632

Jacksonville Office
4151 Woodcock Drive, Suite 217
Jacksonville, FL 32207
(904) 348-2740
Suncom: 870-2740
Fax: (904) 348-2744

Boca Raton Office
8177 West Glades Road, Suite 205
Boca Raton, FL 33434
(407) 451-0996
Suncom: 221-5261
Fax: (407) 451-1905

Miami Office
401 N.W. 2nd Avenue, Suite N-321
Miami, FL 33128
(305) 377-5957
Suncom: 452-5957
Fax: (305) 377-5305

Orlando Office
400 West Robinson Street, Suite N-211
Orlando, FL 32801
(407) 423-6728
Suncom: 344-6728
Fax: (407) 432-6341

Pensacola Office
315-B South Palafox Street
Pensacola, FL 32501
(904) 444-2394
Suncom: 693-2394
Fax: (904) 444-2399

Tampa Office
1313 North Tampa Street, Suite 805
Tampa, FL 33602
(813) 272-3565
Suncom: 571-3565
Fax: (813) 272-3819

GEORGIA

To report suspected worker's compensation fraud, contact:

The Office of the Commissioner of Insurance
Enforcement Division
Floyd Building
Room 704, West Tower
2 Martin Luther King, Jr., Drive
Atlanta, GA 30334
(404) 656-2056

To report suspected fraudulent claims to the appropriate insurance company, call:

The Georgia State Board of Worker's Compensation
Coverage Department
Suite 1000, South Tower
One CNN Center
Atlanta, GA 30303-2788
(404) 656-3692

The Georgia State Board of Worker's Compensation can provide you with the name of the insurance carrier in each specific case so that you can report the suspected fraud directly to the insurance company for investigation.

HAWAII

To report suspected fraud in Hawaii, all allegations must be specific and in writing and sent to the address below for investigation and/or referral to the appropriate insurance company.

Chief - Worker's Compensation Program
Disability Compensation Division
P.O. Box 3769
Honolulu, HI 96812

To report suspected fraud by an insurance company or agent, contact:

> State of Hawaii Insurance Division
> Department of Commerce & Consumer Affairs
> P.O. Box 3614
> Honolulu, HI 96811-3614
> (808) 586-2790

IDAHO

To report suspected fraud against an insurance company, including fraudulent claims, improper billing practices and premium avoidance schemes, contact:

> Fraud Investigation
> Department of Insurance
> 700 West State Street
> Boise, ID 83720
> (208) 334-4250

To report suspected fraudulent claims to the appropriate insurance company, call:

> The Idaho Industrial Commission
> 317 Main
> Boise, ID 83720
> (208) 334-6000
> Attn.: Compensation Consultant Bureau Chief

The Idaho Industrial Commission can provide you with the name of the insurance carrier to each specific case so that you can report the suspected fraud directly to the insurance company for investigation.

To report suspected fraud by an insurance company, agent or broker, contact:

> Compliance and Investigations
> Department of Insurance
> 700 West State Street
> Boise, ID 83720
> (208) 334-4250

ILLINOIS

To report all insurance complaints, including fraud, contact:

> State of Illinois Insurance Department
> Attn.: Complaint Division
> 320 West Washington Street, 4th Floor
> Springfield, IL 62767
> (217) 782-4515

INDIANA

To report all types of worker's compensation fraud, contact:

Insurance Investigations
Indiana Department of Insurance
Suite 300
311 West Washington Street
Indianapolis, IN 46204-2287
(317) 232-2385

IOWA

To report suspected claims fraud, contact:

The Division of Industrial Services
Department of Employment Services
1000 East Grand Avenue
Des Moines, IA 50319
(515) 281-5934

To report suspected agent or insurance company fraud, contact:

Insurance Department of Iowa
Lucas State Office Building, 6th Floor
Des Moines, IA 50319
(515) 281-5705

KANSAS

To report suspected worker's compensation claims fraud, contact:

The Division of Worker's Compensation
600 Merchant Bank Tower
800 S.W. Jackson
Topeka, KS 66612-1227
(913) 296-2996
Attn.: Claims Advisory Section

KENTUCKY

To report suspected fraudulent claims to the appropriate insurance company, call:

The Kentucky Worker's Compensation Board
Perimeter Park West, Building C
1270 Louisville Road
Frankfort, KY 40601
(502) 564-5550

The Kentucky Worker's Compensation Board can provide you with the name of the insurance carrier in each specific case so that you can report the suspected fraud directly to the insurance company for investigation.

To report all insurance complaints, including allegations of worker's compensation fraud, contact:

The Kentucky Department of Insurance
Enforcement Division
P.O. Box 517
Frankfort, KY 40602
(502) 564-3630

LOUISIANA

To report all worker's compensation insurance complaints, including suspected fraud regarding an agent or insurance company contact:

Department of Labor
Office of Worker's Compensation
The Fraud Section
P.O. Box 94040
Baton Rouge, LA 70804-9040
(504) 342-7558

MAINE

To report suspected claims fraud, contact:

The Worker's Compensation Commission
Abuse Investigation Unit
24 Stone Street
Augusta, ME 04330
(207) 289-7078

MARYLAND

To report all types of suspected worker's compensation fraud, including fraud by an agent or insurance company, contact:

The Maryland Insurance Fraud Unit
501 St. Paul Place
Baltimore, MD 21202
(410) 333-8792
1-800-846-4069

To report suspected fraudulent claims to the appropriate insurance company, call:

The Maryland Worker's Compensation Commission
6 North Liberty Street
Baltimore, MD 21201
(410) 333-4700

The Maryland Worker's Compensation Commission can provide you with the name of the insurance carrier in specific cases so that you can report the suspected fraud directly to the insurance company for investigation.

MASSACHUSETTS

To report suspected fraud against an insurance company, including fraudulent claims, improper billing practices and premium avoidance schemes, contact:

The Insurance Fraud Bureau of Massachusetts
(not a state agency)
101 Arch Street, 6th Floor
Boston, MA 02110
(617) 439-0439
In Massachusetts: 1-800-32-FRAUD (1-800-323-7283)

To report suspected fraud by an insurance company, agent or broker, contact:

Division of Insurance
Special Investigations
470 Atlantic Avenue
Boston, MA 02210
(617) 521-7324

MICHIGAN

To report suspected claims fraud, contact:

The Bureau of Worker's Disability Compensation
Department of Labor
P.O. Box 30016
Lansing, MI 48909
(517) 373-3490

MINNESOTA

To report all types of suspected worker's compensation fraud, contact:

Investigative Services Unit
Minnesota Department of Labor and Industry
443 Lafayette Road
St. Paul, MN 55155-4319
(612) 297-5797
Fax: (612) 282-5358

MISSISSIPPI

To report all types of suspected worker's compensation fraud, contact:

Worker's Compensation Commission's Office
P.O. Box 5300
Jackson, MS 39296-5300
(601) 987-4200

MISSOURI

To report all types of suspected worker's compensation fraud, contact:

State of Missouri
Department of Labor and Industry Relations
Division of Worker's Compensation
Fraud and Noncompliance Unit
P.O. Box 58
Jefferson City, MO 65102
Hotline for all worker's compensation matters: 1-800-726-7390

MONTANA

To report all types of suspected worker's compensation fraud including fraud by an agent or insurance company, contact:

Montana Department of Labor and Industry
Employment Relations Division
Standards Bureau
P.O. Box 8011
Helena, MT 59604-8011
WC abuse hotline: 1-800-922-2873
Insurance coverage: 1-800-772-2141

NEBRASKA

To report all types of suspected worker's compensation fraud, contact:

Consumer Affairs Division
State of Nebraska
Department of Insurance
Terminal Building, Suite 400
941 "O" Street
Lincoln, NE 68508
(402) 471-2201

NEVADA

To report suspected worker's compensation claims, employer and provider fraud, contact:

The Office of the Attorney General
Insurance Fraud Section
401 South Third Street, Suite 500
Las Vegas, NV 89101
(702) 486-3420

To report suspected worker's compensation fraud by agents and insurance companies, contact:

Investigation/Enforcement Section
Nevada Department of Insurance
1665 Hot Springs Road, Room 152
Carson City, NV 89710
(702) 687-4270, ext. 338

NEW HAMPSHIRE

To report suspected worker's compensation fraud (including bogus claims, fraud by an agent or insurance company, improper billing, etc.), contact:

The State of New Hampshire
Insurance Department
Property and Casualty Division
169 Manchester Street
Concord, NH 03301
(603) 271-2261

NEW JERSEY

To report all types of suspected worker's compensation fraud, contact:

The Fraud Unit
Department of Insurance
CN 324
Trenton, NJ 08625
(609) 292-8637
Inside New Jersey: 1-800-662-0097

NEW MEXICO

To report any suspected worker's compensation fraud, contact:

The New Mexico Worker's Compensation Administration
Enforcement Bureau
P.O. Box 27198
Albuquerque, NM 87125-7198
(505) 841-6000
Attn.: Fraud Section Supervisor
Inside New Mexico: 1-800-255-7965

NEW YORK

To report any suspected worker's compensation fraud in New York, contact one of the regional offices of the New York Insurance Fraud Bureau, which handles all types of insurance fraud matters. More specific information is as follows:

Statewide hotline for all insurance matters: 1-800-342-3736

New York City area:
New York State Insurance Department
Insurance Fraud Bureau
160 West Broadway
New York, NY 10013
(212) 602-0569

Syracuse area:
New York State Insurance Department
Insurance Fraud Bureau
620 Erie Boulevard West, #105
Syracuse, NY 13204
(315) 423-1102

Albany area:
New York State Insurance Department
Insurance Fraud Bureau
Agency Building 1
The Gov. Nelson A. Rockefeller Empire State Plaza
Albany, NY 12257
(518) 473-0833

Buffalo area:
New York State Insurance Department
Insurance Fraud Bureau
Walter Mahoney State Office Building
65 Court Street, Room 7
Buffalo, NY 14202
(716) 847-7622

NORTH CAROLINA

To report all types of suspected worker's compensation fraud, contact:

North Carolina Industrial Commission
Dobbs Building
430 North Salisbury Street
Raleigh, NC 27611
(919) 733-1953

NORTH DAKOTA

To report all types of suspected worker's compensation fraud, contact:

State of North Dakota
Worker's Compensation Bureau
500 East Front Avenue
Bismarck, ND 58504-5685
(701) 224-3800
Worker's compensation fraud and safety hotline:
1-800-243-3331 (inside North Dakota)

OHIO

To report suspected worker's compensation fraud, contact:

The Ohio Bureau of Worker's Compensation
Fraud Investigations
30 West Spring Street, Level 28
Columbus, OH 43266-0581
Nationwide toll-free fraud hotline: 1-800-837-1554

OKLAHOMA

To report suspected fraudulent claims, including worker's compensation fraud by an agent or insurance company, call:

Office of the Attorney General
Worker's Compensation Fraud Unit
4545 North Lincoln, Suite 260
Oklahoma City, OK 73105
(405) 521-4274
Inside Oklahoma: 1-800-522-8210

The Oklahoma Worker's Compensation Court can provide you with the name of the insurance carrier in each specific case so that you can report the suspected fraud directly to the insurance company for investigation.

OREGON

To report all types of worker's compensation fraud, contact:

> The Investigation Unit
> Compliance Section
> Worker's Compensation Division
> Department of Insurance & Finance
> 440 Labor & Industries Building
> Salem, OR 97310
> (503) 373-1547
> Inside Oregon: 1-800-422-8778

PENNSYLVANIA

To report suspected worker's compensation fraud, including claims, fraud by an agent, broker or insurance company, contact:

> State of Pennsylvania
> Insurance Department
> Bureau of Enforcement
> 1321 Strawberry Square, 13th Floor
> Harrisburg, PA 17120
> (717) 783-2627

RHODE ISLAND

To report suspected worker's compensation claims fraud, contact:

> The Department of Worker's Compensation
> 610 Manton Avenue
> Providence, RI 02909
> (401) 272-0700
> Attn: Education Unit

To report suspected fraud by an insurance company or agent, contact:

> The Department of Business Regulation
> Insurance Division
> 233 Richmond Street, Suite 233
> Providence, RI 02903-4233
> (401) 277-2223

SOUTH CAROLINA

To report suspected fraudulent claims to the appropriate insurance company, call:

The Worker's Compensation Commission
P.O. Box 1715
1612 Marion Street
Columbia, SC 29202-1715
(803) 737-5700
Attn: Claims Department

The South Carolina Worker's Compensation Commission can provide you with the name of the insurance carrier in each specific case so that you can report the suspected fraud directly to the insurance company for investigation.

SOUTH DAKOTA

To report all types of suspected worker's compensation fraud, contact:

The South Dakota Division of Insurance
Department of Commerce & Regulation
500 East Capitol
Pierre, SD 57501-3940 (Mailing Address)
(605) 773-3563

TENNESSEE

To report suspected fraudulent claims to the appropriate insurance company, present all specific information on the case to:

The Division of Worker's Compensation
Department of Labor
710 James Robertson Parkway, 2nd Floor
Nashville, TN 37243-0661
(615) 741-2395

The Tennessee Workers' Compensation Division can provide you with the name of the insurance carrier in each specific case so that you can report the suspected fraud directly to the insurance company for investigation.

To report suspected worker's compensation fraud by an agent or insurance company, contact:

The State of Tennessee
Department of Commerce & Insurance
Property/Casualty Rating Section
500 James Robertson Parkway, 5th Floor
Nashville, TN 37219
(615) 741-2333

TEXAS

To report any suspected worker's compensation fraud, contact:

Insurance Fraud Unit
Texas Department of Insurance
Mail Code 109-3A
P.O. Box 149104
Austin, TX 78714-9104
Toll-free hotline (inside Texas): 1-800-475-4989

UTAH

To report suspected worker's compensation claims fraud, contact:

The Utah Industrial Commission
Industrial Accidents Division
160 East 300 South, 3rd Floor
P.O. Box 146610
Salt Lake City, UT 84114-6610
(801) 530-6800

To report suspected worker's compensation fraud by an agent or insurance company, contact:

The Utah Insurance Department
State Office Building, Room 3110
Salt Lake City, UT 84114
(801) 538-3805
Attn.: Consumer Services

VERMONT

To report suspected worker's compensation claims fraud, contact:

The Department of Labor & Industry
National Life Building
Drawer 20
Montpelier, VT 05620-3401
(802) 828-2286

To report suspected worker's compensation fraud by an agent or insurance company, contact:

> The Department of Banking, Insurance & Securities
> 89 Main Street
> Drawer 20
> Montpelier, VT 05620-3101
> (802) 828-3301
> Attn.: Consumer Services

VIRGINIA

To report suspected worker's compensation fraud by an agent or insurance company, contact:

> State of Virginia
> Worker's Compensation Commission
> 1000 DMV Drive
> Richmond, VA 23220-2036
> (804) 367-8664

WASHINGTON

To report suspected worker's compensation claims fraud, contact:

> The Department of Labor & Industries
> Industrial Insurance Division
> Investigation Section
> P.O. Box 44277
> Olympia, WA 98504-4277
> 1-800-547-8367

To report suspected fraud by an employer or medical provider, contact:

> The Office of the Attorney General
> Chief Investigator/LIFCU
> 900 4th Avenue, 18th Floor
> Seattle, WA 98164
> (206) 389-2029

WEST VIRGINIA

To report all suspected worker's compensation fraud, contact:

> State Bureau of Complaint Programs
> Worker's Compensation Division
> 601 Morris Street
> Charleston, WV 25301
> (304) 558-0131

WISCONSIN

To report suspected fraudulent claims to the appropriate insurance company, call:

> The Worker's Compensation Division
> P.O. Box 7901
> Madison, WI 53707
> (608) 266-1340

The Wisconsin Worker's Compensation Division can provide you with the name of the insurance carrier in each specific case so that you can report the suspected fraud directly to the insurance company for investigation.

To report suspected worker's compensation fraud by an agent or insurance company, contact:

> State of Wisconsin
> Insurance Commissioner's Office
> Complaints Section
> P.O. Box 7873
> Madison, WI 53707-7873
> (608) 266-0103
> In-state toll-free number for all insurance complaints: 1-800-236-8517

WYOMING

To report suspected worker's compensation claims fraud, contact:

> Wyoming Worker's Compensation Division
> Fraudulent Claims Department
> Department of Employment
> 122 West 25th Street
> Herschler Building
> Cheyenne, WY 82002-0700
> (307) 777-7441

About the Authors

Scott Finger is a veteran investigator and surveillance expert. Scott is SIU Director and National Account Manager for InPhoto Surveillance. Scott is also a consultant to insurers on the subject of SIU program management.

Bill Kizorek is the author of 6 books on surveillance and investigations. He is President of InPhoto Surveillance and a consultant to the claims industry, having lectured on 5 continents. He has appeared on national television shows such as, 20/20, Inside Edition and Dateline N.B.C.